GW00683448

The

ASSEMBLY

LIFE

WATCHMAN NEE

Living Stream Ministry
Anaheim, California • www.lsm.org

© 1995 Living Stream Ministry

First Edition, March 1995.

ISBN 978-0-87083-855-2

Published by

Living Stream Ministry
2431 W. La Palma Ave., Anaheim, CA 92801 U.S.A.
P. O. Box 2121, Anaheim, CA 92814 U.S.A.

Printed and bound by CPI Group (UK) Ltd, Croydon, CR0 4YY

11 12 13 14 15 16 / 10 9 8 7 6 5 4 3

CONTENTS

THE ASSEMBLY LIFE

PREFACE TO THE CHINESE EDITION

In recent years, God has raised up many brothers and sisters in various places. As a result of seeing the truth concerning the church, they have gathered together to meet in the Lord's name. They have left human organizations and things that are apart from the Bible, and they have come together to serve the Lord with those who call on the Lord out of a pure heart. For this, we have to thank the Lord.

Although these scattered brothers who are meeting in the Lord's name have seen much concerning human organizations, they do not have, as yet, a deep enough understanding of the Body of Christ. Although they have given up things that should not be in the church, they have not fully lived out the proper living of the Body of Christ. They have dealt with negative things in a thorough way, but they are not thorough with the positive things yet.

Presently, the urgent need of all those who meet in the Lord's name is the truth concerning the practical living of the Body of Christ on earth. The purpose of the publication of this book, *The Assembly Life,* is to meet this need.

This book is a record of a Bible study conducted by Brother Watchman Nee with the local brothers who were meeting in Shanghai after the Third Overcomer Conference in January of this year (together with some out-of-town brothers who stayed behind after the conference). What is covered mainly deals with the practical aspect of our living. The questions and answers are especially appropriate and useful.

The book is divided into four chapters. The first chapter is on the authority in the church. It can be considered as a chapter on the administration of the church. It shows us that God's church is not without organization on earth; it has organization, yet its organization is unlike that of human organizations today. In the church of God, there is no individual freedom and no possibility of independent movement. If ever an organization is firm and strict, it must be the church. God does not want His children to move freely on earth; He rules over His church through the authority He establishes in the church. We should leave human organizations, but at the same time, we should submit to the God-appointed authority. It is right for us to depart from human organizations, but it is wrong for us to overturn the authority that God has established. Yet it is very difficult for us to keep our position and submit to authority. Many people can submit to God, but they cannot submit to the God-appointed authority. However, only those who can submit to the authority appointed by God can submit to God. Whoever does not remain in his position is unlawful, and whoever does not submit to authority is lawless.

The second chapter is on the practice of fellowship. This chapter shows us that there is only one fellowship in the Body of Christ. This matter is very much neglected by the churches today. Many people think that as long as they leave the improper fellowship, the denominations, they have been perfected. Yet if a man only departs from improper things but does not acquire proper things, he has not been perfected. Moreover, unless we return to the proper and unique fellowship of the Body of Christ, all of our fellowship is improper, and our leaving of the denominations merely adds more improper fellowship. All of our fellowship must be the fellowship of the Body of Christ rather than only some local fellowship. We must be able to link up with all the assemblies in the whole world who are meeting in the name of the Lord, instead of practicing a fellowship that is merely bound by a locality. It is true that church affairs should be local, but the fellowship of the church should not be simply local. The fellowship of the church is not local but universal. There should not only be fellowship between individuals, but there should also be fellowship among assemblies.

The third chapter is on the way to meet. This chapter can be considered as a kind of spiritual home education. It shows us the common knowledge a brother or a sister should have concerning various kinds of meetings in a local assembly.

Although spiritual things cannot be taught, there must be proper teachings before there can be a proper living. A proper living comes out of proper teachings.

The fourth chapter is on the boundary of a local assembly. This chapter deals with the delineation of the boundary of a local assembly. The Bible shows us that God has appointed the city as the unit of a church. The boundary of a local church is determined by the boundary of the city to which it belongs. This God-ordained way maintains the balance in the fellowship of the assemblies in the various places, and it avoids much trouble and confusion. We should not randomly choose from among the few assemblies around us and freely meet there. Rather, we should decide on the place to meet based on the locality in which we belong. If we are in one city, we should not meet with an assembly in another city. Even if the place of meeting in the other city is closer than the place of meeting in our own city, we should still meet in our own city, rather than the other city. If this is not our practice, the fellowship among all the assemblies will not be balanced, and confusion will result. God does not want us to have freedom of movement. Even in the matter of choosing where to meet, God does not allow us to have a fleshly preference and choice.

May God bless this book so that it becomes the light of life to God's children everywhere, not ordinances in letters. "To Him be the glory in the church and in Christ Jesus unto all the generations forever and ever. Amen."

Witness Lee
Shanghai
September 10, 1934

INTRODUCTION

(A Bible Study Given in Shanghai
February 19-26, 1934)

Brothers and sisters, although this meeting is in the nature of a Bible study, we cannot read all the scriptural references because of the limitation of time. We can only read the references as we come to them. During the Saturday evening brothers' meeting, we considered what we should study. The decision that evening was that we should study the matter of the assembly life. Before we study this subject, I would first ask the brothers and sisters to consider the importance of this matter.

During the past conference, we saw that before times eternal, God had a will and a foreordained plan of His own. His goal is to have a group of people containing His life who are like His Son. The goal of God was to establish not just the individual Christ, but also the corporate Christ. This corporate Christ is the church. From this we can know that it is the church which God pays attention to today. Unfortunately, it is not only the carnal believers who fail to emphasize what God stresses, but even the spiritual believers fail to emphasize it. They always replace the church of God with many works.

Today what Satan causes man to do is substitute the church of God with various kinds of work. However, we know that the purpose of God from beginning to end is to have a corporate Christ, which is the church, so that Christ might be the Head and the believers might be the members. Satan is determined to destroy this plan. This is why he causes man to pursue various works in order to replace the church.

Today some lay much stress on preaching the gospel, and by so doing they replace the church with gospel preaching. There are many today who can surely preach the gospel and save sinners. And preaching the gospel is good, but if gospel preaching replaces the church and causes men never to think about the church, then we are definitely deceived by Satan. What I have said is not too strong. God's intention in gospel preaching is merely to collect stones for the church. If gospel preaching substitutes for the church, that is wrong.

There are some who establish missions, encourage foreign evangelism, zealously donate money, form national councils, set up organizations for foreign evangelism, and send missionaries to foreign lands for evangelistic work. But why do many people today know only missions and not the church? The reason is because from eternity past God's emphasis was the church, but man's emphasis in this age is missions. Many have forgotten the church! Mr. Gordon has said, "God never sets up missions; He only establishes the church." However, men today set up mission boards, evangelistic organizations, schools, hospitals, humanistic societies, orphanages, charitable associations (as the Methodist Episcopal Church does), and even Sunday schools to help others. Are these good or bad? They are good, but if man uses these to replace the church of God, God will never be satisfied. Do you see Satan's craftiness? Satan's subtle method is to utilize works used by God and substitute them for the church, which God in His eternal will intends to establish. If your eyes are open, you will see that all these things should be dropped and that you should turn your attention to the church, because the church life, the life of the Body of Christ, is the goal of God.

Many Christians may say, "We have not established mission boards, humanistic societies, Sunday schools, schools, and hospitals." Please do not speak so fast. You may not have done these wrong things on the negative side, but what have you done on the positive side? Many would think, "As long as I am zealous, victorious, and a holy Christian, that is good enough." Brothers and sisters, I say a strong word; these are not what God is after; they are not His unique goal. I am by no means saying that zeal, victory, and holiness are insignificant. These are significant, but they are not God's ultimate goal. What God desires is the corporate church, the building, the spiritual house. He is not after fragmentary or individual pieces of brick, tile, wood, or stone. God desires a body, not a finger or any other member. What God wants is the church. His desire is for Christ to have the preeminence in the church and to be Head of the church as well. Although wood, stone, brick, and tile are necessary, they are by no means the goal of God. You have been a Christian for these many years, but how much time have you spent considering what God is after? Have you ever thought about this matter of the church? Or has your primary attention been paid to how to pray, how to overcome sin, how to help sinners be saved, and how to study the Bible well? Do you only think about these things, or have you really considered what the church is? What God wants is a church. Anything that falls short of this fails to meet the goal of God. I am by no means saying that these other things are not good, but I am saying that anything short of the church cannot be counted as the goal of God. If Sunday schools are merely for the sake of Sunday schools, orphanages merely for orphanages, humanistic societies merely for humanistic societies, and gospel preaching merely for gospel preaching, it is fine as long as they do not replace the church. For all these things fall short of the church of God. What God wants is the church. The death of the Lord Jesus was for the church, and the coming of the Holy Spirit was also for the church. From beginning to end, in the New Testament, one principle can be found: Everything is for the church. Take, for example, the fact that the Lord's death was for the church. The book of Ephesians tells us, "Christ also loved the church and gave Himself up for her." The Lord was raised from the dead to be far above all rule and authority, and He is above all to be Head over all things to the church. The Lord builds the church on this rock. The work of the Holy Spirit for the past two thousand years has been for the building up of the church. God saves sinners and enables men to overcome in order to establish the church. It is for the building up of the church that God has given us apostles, prophets, evangelists, shepherds, and teachers. Ephesians tells us that the Lord cleanses the church by the washing of water in the word and sanctifies her in order that He might present her to Himself a glorious church, not having spot or wrinkle or any such things, but that she should be holy and without blemish. Here again it is a matter of the church. God's ultimate goal is to have the New Jerusalem, and what the New Jerusalem typifies is the church. God's goal as recorded in the Old Testament, New Testament, the four Gospels, and Revelation is to have the New Jerusalem, which is for the church. I say strongly that unless our aim, work, and living today are for the church—that is, for the accomplishment of what God is after—we are a big failure. May the Lord have mercy on us and deliver us from our limited vision into His goal and into what He emphasizes in the Scriptures.

We come together every Lord's Day morning and afternoon to listen to messages, and we come together every Lord's Day evening to break the bread. Can we be considered good believers just by doing this? Or should we pursue being good brothers or good sisters by trying to render help to the meeting and the church? Now I will narrow myself down from this broad realm to smaller matters. The broad principles have been covered in the conference. Now we will cover only small matters. We will pay attention to the matter of practice and not spiritual principles. We will only mention the outward matters of the church. We cannot cover the spiritual implications of these things at this time. As to the life of Christ and the Body of Christ, we may speak more about them in the future when the opportunity arises.

The church is God's goal. Today He places this goal before man. God's ultimate desire is to have the New Jerusalem. God intends to put the church, which is represented by the New Jerusalem, into every city as a unit. Before the New Jerusalem descends from heaven, God's goal is to have a miniature of the New Jerusalem in every city. This means that God desires to have a church in every city to express His eternal will. From beginning to end, the most important work God desires to do is to build up the Body of Christ. For this reason God establishes a local church in every city. The local church is the miniature of the magnificent church of God, a small-scale model expressing the New Jerusalem. The will of God is to establish the church, the Body of Christ, the New Jerusalem. But this scope is too vast; how can we touch the New

Jerusalem, which is in the new heaven and new earth? What shall we do? We can never grasp this firmly. However, you can come to Shanghai to achieve this purpose. For in every city there is a miniature where God puts the saved ones and unites and assembles them together to become a local church and thereby express His will.

If you want to go on a big steamer to travel to a foreign country, you must first ask the officers of the ship for the directions to your cabin. Once you board the ship, it is as if you are in a big city, and you will not know where to find your cabin. Therefore, you have to ask the officers to show you the way in detail. They may show you a miniature model of the ship which has the same structure as the actual steamer. They may remove the decks layer by layer and show you how to go to your cabin step by step. After seeing this, you will have a clear sense of direction. When you board the ship again, you will be able to easily find your cabin. The New Jerusalem in God's eternal purpose is big, while the churches He establishes in every city are small. They are miniature manifestations of God's purpose. We will study the things concerning these miniature manifestations. In other words, we will study the things related to the assembly. If we do not do this, we will miss the big things and also fail in the small things.

I am not here accusing you! I myself am guilty! In these many years of evangelistic work in China, very few have paid attention to God's emphasis. Roman Catholicism has been in China for more than three hundred years, and if we count from Nestorianism, Christianity has been in China for over a thousand years. Yet no one has ever paid attention to the expression of the eternal will of God on a small scale. But we also are the same. We only pay attention to personal victory over sins, overcoming experiences, work, and saving souls, but we have not yet seen how to express in a particular locality God's will concerning the church. May God be gracious to us and cause us to see that personal victory over sins, overcoming experiences, and the work of saving souls are merely things related to the local assemblies—they should not replace the church. God's center is fixed on the church in every locality, and everything else should be joined to this center. Therefore, our aim today is not merely to pay attention to overcoming experiences, victory over sin, preaching the gospel to sinners, and having prayers answered. Rather, we should go a step further and ask what we should do in order to be fitly framed together with other brothers and sisters.

Fukien is famous for its stonework. The workmanship of the Fukien stone workers lies in their ability to cut uneven and odd stones into smooth and orderly pieces and put them together. The cut stones are not like the stones on Kuling Mountain, which are roughly mixed together to form walls. Each stone in the workers' hands is finely cut and pieced together. Although they are different sizes and shapes, they are joined together and match one another. The question today is not whether this piece of stone is good or bad, big or small, beautiful or ugly, but whether this piece of stone is properly fitted with other pieces of stone and whether these pieces of stone can be built into a house. Many Christians today are very good, and others are extremely shining and beautiful, but they cannot be framed together. They are either too big or too tall; they just cannot be fitly framed with other Christians. Every person who is saved is a living stone. Therefore, the question is not whether you are victorious, defeated, powerful, weak, good, or bad. The question is whether you can be joined with all the other living stones, properly fitted into the building. If you are a stone which leaves cracks between you and the other stones, you are not of much use in the house of God.

During these few days, our study will concentrate on the things related to the assembly life. Everything outside of the assembly life, such as the brothers' relationship with one another, mutual forgiveness, etc., has been covered during the past few Lord's Day mornings and afternoons. All other points concerning our corporate life together will be covered in future messages on the Lord's Day morning and afternoon. Presently, we will pay attention to how brothers ought to behave in the meetings as good brothers and how sisters ought to behave as good sisters. Therefore, we have decided to study the following subjects: the authority of the church, the fellowship of the church, the way to meet, the way to divide up our local assembly into one meeting on Wen-teh Lane and another meeting on Gordon Lane, and how the two are one.

I hope that the brothers realize that in this meeting we do not want just one person giving the message. At any time questions can be raised. Every brother can ask questions. But when you ask questions, your voice should be loud. If you want to be a good brother, you must love the brothers' ears and not your own throat.

CHAPTER ONE

AUTHORITY IN THE CHURCH

In order to understand authority in the church, we must first understand what authority is. Otherwise, we will not understand authority in the church.

What is authority? In the whole universe, nothing is harder to understand than authority. Two things are very difficult to explain in the Bible: glory and authority. Many people can understand holiness, righteousness, and patience; they may comprehend these matters a little. But what is God's glory, and what is God's authority? Man cannot understand them and explain them. God's glory is related to God Himself, while God's authority is related to His government. God Himself is glorious, while His government is executed through His authority. God's authority was the principle by which He organized the universe. He rules the universe through authority. (Today, we will only mention the matter of authority in brief. We will wait for another day to discuss the subject in detail.) How did God create the heavens and the earth? He created by His authority. How did God restore this world? He restored by His authority also. On the first day when God created light, He did not gather all of the electricity together and make light; He only gave a command and said, "Let there be light," and there was light. The second day God said, "Let there be the firmament," and there was the firmament. God commanded with His word, and He acted according to His authority. He did not act according to His power or His ways. His word signifies His command, which represents His authority. Can you see that God only exercised His authority? God created the universe with His authority, and He rules the universe with His authority. Both the beginning of the universe and the maintenance of the universe are the result of God's authority.

In the beginning, after the universe was created, God

appointed a cherubim as the archangel to rule over everything. God was over everything, and He ruled over the spirit-endowed animals and over all things through the archangel, the cherubim. Sin is lawlessness, and lawlessness is just the overthrowing of God's authority. Lawlessness was the reason the archangel fell and became Satan and also the reason sin entered the universe. The archangel attempted to overturn God's authority because he desired to uplift himself to become equal with God. Sin entered the world because Eve would not submit to Adam. She acted without Adam's command and ate the fruit of the tree of the knowledge of good and evil.

Although the world is filled with sin today, authority is still the principle of God's government. In many things, we can see God's appointed authority. For example, wives should submit to their husbands, servants to their masters, students to their teachers, citizens to the officers, and subordinates to their superiors. All of this is ordained by God. God desires that man submit to authority because the authorities are not only appointed by God, but they also represent God. This is why Romans clearly says that there is no authority except God. Therefore, no Christian student should boycott classes, no Christian worker should strike, no Christian children should dishonor their parents, and no Christian citizen should engage in a revolution. If anyone does these things, he is not just overturning those he directly opposes, he is overturning God's authority. God created the universe with His authority, and He maintains the universe with His authority. What is sin? It is lawlessness—refusing to submit to authority. "Sin is lawlessness" (1 John 3:4). Both Satan and Adam overturned God's authority; by this both sinned. Whoever does not recognize authority and submit to authority is a lawless one, and he has sinned.

Many believers have never realized such a wonderful thing as authority. Yet if a man wants to be a good believer, he has to know what authority is. Authority represents God. If one traces authority to its ultimate source, he will see that authority is just God. Therefore, a Christian must not only submit to the head of a nation or to all its ministers, but he must submit even to a policeman on the street because the latter has authority. He represents not only the government, but God as well. You cannot despise him just because he earns a few dollars a month. Authority is something that issues from God. The Bible is very strict about this matter. Paul, Peter, and Jude all said that we should not revile those in high position. Therefore, in our conversation, we cannot accuse or criticize the head of our government. It is difficult for a Christian to be an editor of a newspaper because one can hardly avoid criticizing the superiors in political commentary.

The book of Jude records the incident of Michael arguing with the devil over the body of Moses. Michael dared not revile Satan. He would only say, "The Lord rebuke you," because he was once the subordinate of Satan. There was a time when Michael was under his authority. Therefore, Michael only said, "The Lord rebuke you." He would not speak on his own; he only invoked an authority higher than Satan's—God's authority. He knew what authority was. Therefore, he dared not revile Satan himself.

When our Lord was on earth, He was also fully under authority. During His youth, He was under the authority of His parents, and He kept all the ordinances. He was the Creator. Yet He was limited by every one of man's limitations. He told His mother, "Did you not know that I must be in the things of My Father?" (Luke 2:49). If we were there, we would not have gone home with our parents. But the Lord was different; He went back with them. When He began to work, He was under the authority of the government. During His trial, He was still under the authority of the government. He did not revile the government; rather, He allowed it to do whatever it wanted to do to Him. We can see that no one has ever been as submissive to authority as our Lord.

Once when Paul was judged and stood before the court, he willingly submitted to the authority there. When the high priest's accusations became too much, Paul said, "God is going to strike you, you whitewashed wall" (Acts 23:3). When the others rebuked him for reviling God's high priest, Paul became quiet and allowed them to accuse him. According to the Bible, nothing is greater and more important than the matter of authority.

The other side of authority is submission. Therefore, the Bible mentions authority, on the one hand, and submission, on the other hand. The Bible also pays considerable attention to the matter of submission. Submission and authority are related one to the other. If a man submits, he comes under God's authority. Otherwise, he overturns God's authority.

In the church God has also appointed His authority, and we should submit to this authority. In the world, in the community, and in our homes, we should submit to authority. God has ordained us to do one thing, which is to submit to authority. We have to lay hold of this one point: whoever wants to overturn any authority overturns God. Do not think that we can submit to God and, at the same time, disobey our parents, husbands, superiors, headmasters, principals, or other men with authority. There is no such thing. If we cannot submit to God's appointed authority on earth, we can never submit to God. In the same way, those who cannot submit to authority in the church cannot submit to God.

I am afraid that many brothers and sisters have come to meet with us for different reasons. Some have come for the purpose of practicing mutual love and mutual care. This, of course, is very good. But we have to realize that we are not without authority among us. There is authority among us, and we ought to submit to authority. Christians often think that once they leave the denominations, they can act as they please. They think that we are all the same and that no one can rebuke anyone else. They think that they can be lawless Christians. Actually, we have to realize that if we leave the denominations just because we want to be free from any kind of control or domination, this kind of presumptuous leaving of the denominations is a big mistake. Those who come to meet with us have to know that we are more bound by authority.

There are three reasons that a man leaves a denomination: (1) He is disappointed in the denominations. For example, he may expect to become a pastor. However, when his wish is not fulfilled, he disagrees and leaves. (2) He does not have freedom in the denominations. He feels that he is limited and controlled by men, and he thinks that by leaving the denominations, he can be a free evangelist. He will not have to take a salary and be controlled by men, and he can act according to his own wish. Actually, before God there is no such thing as a free evangelist. Today, we only have the Body life. We are restricted by the church and do not have any freedom of our own. (3) He sees the divisiveness in the denominations and that divisions are of the flesh. *At the same time,* he may see the Body of Christ and realize that everything he does has to be limited by the brothers and that he should learn to be a member in the Body. (Yet many people do not see the Body. They have merely left a big denomination and become a small denomination in themselves. They have not seen that they should be restricted among the brothers and sisters.)

Of the three kinds of people mentioned above, only the third kind is right in God's eyes. God's goal is to have the Body life and to take away all independent movement. God has His authority in the church, and He desires to manifest His authority in the church. Therefore, every member should learn to submit to God's authority and be restricted by the other members. Therefore, on the negative side, every brother should see how wrong denominationalism is, but on the positive side, he should see that there are no independent activities in the Body life.

THE AUTHORITY IN THE CHURCH

How should authority in the church be assigned? God has appointed the elders and apostles to be the authority in the church. In each respective church, God establishes elders; among all the churches, God establishes apostles. The authority of apostles is for overseeing all the churches, while the authority of elders is for overseeing each respective local church. In order to manifest His authority in the church, God appoints elders in each of the local churches to represent His authority. Another name for elders is *overseers,* which bears the connotation of authority. The Bible tells us to submit to these ones because they represent authority. All authorities are there to represent God. Therefore, the authority of the elders is for representing and expressing God's authority. It does not matter if an elder is a good representation or a bad one. One should submit to the elders as long as the authority is from God. Whoever does not submit to the authority of the church has lost his standing as a brother.

In the early meetings of a local church, there are no elders. Later, some who bear some resemblance of an elder are gradually manifested. Eldership and overseership are two designated names for the same office. An elder refers to the person, while an overseer refers to the function of such a person. Moreover, in the Bible, elders are always plural in number. There is never just one elder, because it is necessary for the spirits of two to three persons to receive the same leading in order to be assured that what they are doing is right. Individualism is not a scriptural principle, and it easily leads to errors.

HOW GOD APPOINTS ELDERS

How does God appoint elders? In an assembly, there are always a few brothers whose growth is more obvious than the others'. They bear a more excellent testimony than others and are desirous of picking up the work of an elder. They also bear some resemblance of an elder. As a result, the apostles appoint them to be elders to oversee the brothers. The church in Ephesus gives us an example of this. In the beginning, there were only saved believers in Ephesus; no elders were appointed. But after the apostles went there the second time, we see elders there. The first time Paul went out from Antioch, his intention was merely to save some people. But later, he appointed elders in every city (Acts 14:23). Before a meeting is properly established as an assembly, it is still feeble in its walk, and there is the need for others to support it. But after some are able to take up the responsibility of overseership, the apostles appoint them to be elders.

At times, the apostles could not appoint elders personally; they then sent others to do the appointing. Timothy and Titus were this kind of people. According to the direction of the apostle, they went to different cities and appointed elders, who then bore the responsibility of the local churches.

Since the appointment of the elders is for the purpose of representing God's authority, the elders should understand that Christ is the Head and that the church is here to express His heart's desire. The elders should inquire concerning the Lord's desire. Only then will they be able to express Christ's authority in the meetings. Through these ones, God makes the decision to move or stop. Therefore, all the brothers should learn to submit to these ones. Of course, no one likes to see anyone lording it over him. Although the elders should not lord it over us, we should submit to the God-appointed authority as our part. God has ordained two things in eternity: authority and submission. But many believers do not like to submit to authority. The world is filled with lawlessness today. I am afraid that the mystery of this lawlessness has become manifest in the church. Parents are criticized at will by children, and husbands submit to the authority of their wives. Headmasters and teachers are attacked, opposed, and elected by students, and workers strike at will. Such things are happening frequently. Now is the time that lawless ones will appear as the Bible predicted. If we are not careful, and if we refuse to submit to authority, we are not following Christ but following Antichrist instead. If we cannot submit to authority, how can we expect others to submit to authority? When those who receive a salary from the so-called churches come to rule over us, we cannot submit to them. But if God has placed a certain person in a certain position and has charged us to submit to him, we should submit accordingly. We should obey the ones who watch over our souls as those who will render an account (Heb. 13:17). Therefore, submission to the elders is something that no one can overturn. Hebrews 13:17 Obey the ones leading you and submit to them, for they watch over your souls as those who will render an account, that they may do this with joy and not groaning; for this would be unprofitable to you.

THE TITLE AND THE APPOINTMENT
OF ELDERS AMONG US

Let us summarize: (1) The elders are the overseers; (2) the eldership is plural in number; and (3) the elders are appointed by the apostles or the ones sent by the apostles. We know that there are no apostles today and that there is no one sent by the apostles. How then can elders be produced?

In the course of our discussion in the brothers' meeting, concerning biblical questions among the co-workers, we have agreed on the following judgment, according to the Bible and the teaching of the Holy Spirit: presently, due to the fact that there are no apostles, there is no possibility for official elders to be appointed. We cannot confer on anyone the title of an elder. If the title of an elder is conferred, we would have to ask where are the apostles who appointed these elders? However, we are not saying that no one is doing the work of an elder. Although we do not have the official title of an elder, we can find men in all the places who resemble elders and who are doing the work of an elder. They serve as elders in an unofficial way. How can this group of people be raised up to do the work of an elder? Who appointed them to be "unofficial" elders? They have been appointed by "unofficial" apostles.

Today, it is a fact that we do not have apostles among us. However, there are a group of people who are doing the work of the apostles, such as preaching the gospel and establishing churches. They readily admit that they cannot match the apostles in their holiness, power, victory, and work. They are merely doing a small part of the work of the apostles, perhaps only a thousandth part. Today, God is working through this group of people in the same way that He was working through the apostles in the early days. Formerly, the apostles established churches everywhere. Today, this group of people are establishing churches everywhere. We admit that they are far inferior to the apostles and are not qualified to be called apostles. Yet we cannot deny that they are doing part of the work of the apostles. This group of people are the apostles God uses today in this time of the church's degradation.

God saves sinners and gathers believers through this group of people. They are the most suitable group to lead those who are under their care to respect certain ones in their meetings and consider them as the "elders" among them.

We are merely helping the brothers to submit to these ones. We have to be careful. If we are not careful, we can easily fall into the Catholic system of apostolic succession or the teaching of the Methodist Episcopal Church, which asserts that bishops have apostolic authority. Our judgment is not only according to the scriptural teaching, but this judgment fully matches our experience. For example, Brother Chu is working in Putung and has saved some people there. If he asks Brother Hwang to go there to appoint elders, Brother Hwang would not know whom to appoint because only Brother Chu knows the local situation. He has been continually leading the believers and feeding them. Only he understands the spiritual condition of the local brothers and is concerned about their souls. Only he can lead them to submit to the ones who act as elders among them. At the same time, the rest of the brothers should learn to accept God's appointed authority.

We cannot refuse submission to authority. We have to ask God to humble us. If we cannot be an "elder," we should submit to others who are the "elders." We should learn to be submissive persons. If our flesh has been deeply judged, we will consider submission to be a good thing and an easy matter; we will consider submission to be something sweet. As long as the flesh is not judged, the church will never be proper. If the brothers deal with the flesh properly and are willing to submit, no difficulty will arise. Therefore, those who are doing the work of the apostles should lead the brothers to acknowledge the ones who should be appointed as "elders" and help the brothers submit to these "elders."

THE QUALIFICATIONS OF AN ELDER

In the Bible, there are clear guidelines concerning the qualifications of the elders. They must be able to rule themselves and manage their own family, and they must know how to deal with outsiders. They must have much assurance concerning God's truth and must be able to teach it. We will list the qualifications as follows:

(1) Ruling themselves. Why does a person have to rule himself? When a person cannot rule his own temper, he cannot manage the church of God. Subduing one's own heart and spirit is the most difficult thing to do. If a man cannot submit to the authority of Christ, he cannot make others submit to Christ's authority. In 1 Timothy and Titus, the words

concerning an elder not being one who drinks excessively, or who strikes others, etc., refer to the aspect of the self-control of an elder. In short, an elder must be one who can rule himself.

Self-Control In addition, an elder must be the husband of one woman. All those who have had concubines cannot be an elder because this means that such a person cannot control himself.

(2) Managing one's own house. If a man cannot manage his own house, he cannot manage the church. If he cannot manage his own children, how can he manage the brothers? The eldership is a position; it is not a gift. Teachers, shepherds, and evangelists are gifts. But eldership refers to a person's position in the church. Therefore, such a person must be experienced and capable. His house is his testing ground. If he cannot make his wife and children submit to him at home, and if he cannot be a good husband or a good father, he cannot be a good elder in the church. In dealing with his own wife and children, God puts him to the test to see if he can deal with the brothers and sisters.

At the same time, God also uses our job and the things related to our office, school, and hospital as a test. If a man is efficient at his business, in managing a school, in conducting himself in his office, and in directing his children and servants, he can manage the church well. If a man cannot manage these things, he cannot possibly manage God's church in a proper way.

(3) Having a good public testimony. An elder is a person who represents the church. Sometimes an elder has to represent the assembly to deal with outsiders. If he does not have a good testimony, the whole church will be slandered. When a person has a bad reputation in public testimony it does not necessarily mean that he is bad. However, if a person has a good reputation in public, it surely means that he is somewhat good. Therefore, a good reputation is important, while a bad name does not necessarily mean much. In this world, men primarily say bad things about others; few say good things about others. The Chinese say that those who are in the public eye are "under ten eyes and under ten fingers." Few people say good things about others. Most people tend to

destroy the reputations of others. If men can find something good to say about a person and give good marks to him, then he surely must be somewhat good. If a greedy, self-centered, and defiled son of Adam can call a Christian a good man, then the Christian surely must be good.

(4) Having much assurance in the truth of God. Since the work of an elder is related to the church and not to a worldly organization, he needs to have much assurance in God's truth. To do other things, it is not absolutely necessary to have a good reputation or to have much assurance in the truth; one does not need to be apt at teaching the Bible to do other things. Yet an elder must be apt to teach the brothers and sisters. An elder is a doorkeeper of the church. What happens when all the brothers want to preach? The elders must consider who should preach and who should not preach. They should find out who are flippant ones, undesirable ones, and incapable ones. They should be able to render the brothers much encouragement as well as discouragement. If they do not have much assurance in the truth, they will think that all the brothers are equally good and that everyone can preach. In this way, they will be men of no discernment.

At the same time, an elder must be one who can differentiate and judge. He should be able to judge the kind of teachings that should be introduced to the church and the kind of teachings that should be rejected. If the elders do this, the brothers will not become confused in the messages they hear. (For a detailed discussion of the above qualifications of an elder, see 1 Tim. 3 and Titus 1.)

THE RESPONSIBILITIES OF THE ELDERS

(1) The elders are the overseers. The Bible calls the elders the overseers. The work of an overseer is to oversee, which is to observe from above. In particular it means to detect the dangers that are coming to an assembly and to be aware ahead of time of the dangers that may come to individual brothers or to the whole assembly. Among us, we have many brothers and sisters. It is hard to avoid problems or weaknesses or to be free from sin, discord, dishonesty, failure to repay loans, disgraces, or scandals in dealing with outsiders.

When these things happen, the responsible brothers or those who are doing the work of an elder should step forward, to deal with such matters. They should not allow the leaven to enter the assembly. These unofficial elders should deal with all these shady matters among the brothers. This is their responsibility. They should come to your house to ask about these matters and deal with them. When they come into your house, you should submit to their decision because their decision is the Lord's decision; their authority is the Lord's authority.

The authority asserted by the Catholic Church is too much. Its failure lies in its outward practice. However, the inward reality of their proposal is correct. The problem is that they only have the outward form without the inward reality. If they had the inward reality, they would be right. They would have the proper authority if they were joined to the source in exercising their authority.

(2) The elders express opinions and make judgments on various matters. Only the elders can express their opinion concerning certain matters. No brother can stand up in the meeting at will to express his opinion concerning what to believe and what not to believe. If any brother does such a thing, he is overturning the authority of the elders. Therefore, only the elders have the authority to judge, utter declarations or announcements that are directed toward the public, and make judgments concerning disputes in truths; this is not the work of ordinary brothers. An ordinary believer can only speak on his own behalf. An elder can speak on behalf of the whole church. This is because he is under the Head and is speaking on behalf of the church. This relates to the order in the church.

(3) The elders manage the matters and meetings related to the sisters. In the Bible, we see only brothers as elders; we do not see sisters as elders. The place God has assigned for the sisters is to be under someone's ruling; they do not have a place in ruling over others. God does not allow women to manage the church. In the Bible, there are deacons and deaconesses, but there are no female elders. This shows that in managing the affairs of the church, God wants the man to

be the head of the woman. Therefore, the sisters should learn to submit by the grace of God. If there are some among the sisters who can serve others, they can do the work of this service. But if anything needs to be decided, the decisions should be made by those who are responsible as the elders. For example, if some among the sisters want to be baptized or be received for the bread breaking meeting, the sisters can testify for them, but the final decision rests with the elders. Some sisters may have the gifts and may be respected by other brothers and sisters, but the question of position and authority is more important in the Bible than the question of gift, and the question of God's truth is more important than the question of ability. Suppose the sisters would like to have a sisters' meeting at 4:30 p.m. on Saturday. The sisters can express their opinion and check with the responsible brothers. If the brothers think that this is proper, they will not stop it and will allow the sisters to meet accordingly. If the sisters do this, they are not acting independently but properly and in oneness. This shows that their meetings are not private meetings but meetings of the church.

Why do the sisters have to follow this procedure? The reason is that the sisters tend to be emotional and are easily deceived. The elders are there to protect the sisters. If everything concerning the church is decided by the brothers, the sisters will be protected and preserved in their covered position, and they will avoid many problems.

Every problem that arises is corporate in nature and is not the problem of an individual. The elders have a responsibility to properly oversee the matters related to the sisters. While the sisters are standing on the ground of submission through submission to Christ's authority, the elders should not shun their responsibility through fear of offending the sisters or of arousing suspicion. Of course, there are limits to the authority of the elders. But we must not forget that Barak was before Deborah and became the head covering to Deborah (see Judg. 4:4-7).

(4) The elders should manage the matters related to the church meetings and preaching. The elders should control and forbid errors that may arise in the church. For example, in the

meeting, some brothers may stand up to say some improper words. Those who do not have the gift of teaching desire to speak many times; it seems as if they are addicted to preaching. Those who have the gifts, on the other hand, do not like to speak and would rather hide themselves. Therefore, when the elders notice that men who are not suitable to conduct Bible study or to preach are trying to do these things, they should stop them. If some brothers pray, preach, or give announcements in an improper way, the elders should notify them after the meeting, explain their mistakes to them, and forbid them from doing similar things again. If the elders do not do this, these brothers will go on with their behavior. You may think that you should be patient with these ones. But the weaker ones will not be able to stand them. For this reason, you have to take up the responsibility to notify them.

Please understand that there is not a strict organization among us. Even when believers who have not left the denominations request to be received, we receive them. Our door is wide open. Everyone in the denominations who is saved can come and break bread with us. Suppose that some of them purposely try to entice some of our brothers and sisters to join them in their Bible study in their homes, after breaking bread with us, or suppose that they gather some of the brothers and sisters who are meeting with us to listen to their opinionated doctrines. When this happens, the church will be divided through their speaking. Whenever things of this nature occur, any brother or sister should report it to the "elders." We must wait until the responsible brothers announce in the meeting that certain people will have meetings in their homes before we can all go. Otherwise, these kinds of meetings in the homes should not be held. It does not mean that we have no personal liberty. But we should submit to God's authority and control and enjoy the liberty of the limitations of the meetings. Our familiarity with certain persons often brings in leaven through conversations with them, and a sect is formed which endangers the whole lump. Therefore, the brothers have to pay attention to this matter, learn to submit to authority, and not do things that the elders have not endorsed.

(5) The elders make decisions concerning the Lord's Day meeting and write letters of recommendation. Whether the Lord's Day meeting should be held in the morning or in the afternoon is a matter to be decided by the elders. The writing of a letter of recommendation is also not something that every brother can do. Sometimes, you may write a letter recommending a person to the brothers in another locality. However, only letters written by the elders can represent the church. This shows once again that the elders represent the whole church. They are responsible for overseeing the church and keeping the church from trouble. Therefore, the elders have to learn to serve properly and exercise their authority properly, while the brothers have to learn to submit.

(6) The elders are the patterns. After the elders are appointed and acknowledged, they should be respected by the brothers. At the same time, the elders themselves should take up their responsibility with fear and trembling. They should consider themselves as having no authority. The Bible tells us these two aspects of the truth in a wonderful way. To the brothers and sisters, the elders represent God's authority, and everyone should submit to them. But to the elders themselves, they have no authority. After hearing about the authority of the elders, are we not afraid that the elders may misuse their authority? What would happen if they began to lord it over us? But God tells the elders, "Therefore the elders among you...shepherd the flock of God among you, overseeing not under compulsion but willingly, according to God...nor as lording it over your allotments but by becoming patterns of the flock" (1 Pet. 5:1-3). The elders do not have any authority in themselves; they only have the authority of God. If you are in Christ, understand God's heart, and are able to tell others about God's heart, you are the true authority. The elders should not lord it over the flock. They should be careful to submit to God's authority and be a pattern to the flock. Only then can they demonstrate their authority to the brothers and sisters. On the one hand, the brothers should submit to Christ's authority, which the elders represent. On the other hand, the elders themselves should realize that they have no authority in themselves and that they are there merely as

patterns. (Concerning the authority of the elders, please see the books of 1 Timothy, Titus, and Acts 20.)

(7) Accusations against the elders. The books of Timothy tell us, "Against an elder receive not an accusation, but before two or three witnesses" (1 Tim. 5:19, KJV). In this matter, we should pay attention to two points. First, there must be a written accusation; words from the mouth do not count because many times words alone are groundless and can easily be denied or changed. Second, there must be two or three witnesses; the testimony of one is not reliable. In the Bible, two or three witnesses constitute the word of testimony. The apostles and those whom they have specifically assigned should be responsible for handling such accusations. I would draw your attention again to the fact that because there are no official apostles today, there are no official elders. There is only a group of people who are doing a part of the work that the apostles did at the beginning. Since they are responsible for appointing elders, they are also responsible for dealing with elders.

THE RELATIONSHIP BETWEEN AN ELDER
AND OTHER ELDERS OF OTHER LOCALITIES

God's gifts transcend local boundaries, but position is strictly related to the locality. God's gifts, such as the evangelists, shepherds, and teachers, can function anywhere because these gifts are given by God to the whole church (Eph. 4), and they are for all the local assemblies. No worker can rule over any one particular congregation, as pastors do today in the denominations. In the Bible one cannot find such a thing. If you can edify the believers in Shanghai, you can also edify the believers in northern Kiangsu. If you are a teacher, you can teach the Bible in Shanghai and also teach the Bible in northern Kiangsu, Nanking, or Tsinan. You will never lose your ability as a teacher by moving to another place. If you are an evangelist, you can preach the gospel in Shanghai, and you can preach the gospel in northern Kiangsu, Nanking, or Tientsin. If you cannot preach the gospel in Shanghai, you cannot preach the gospel anywhere else. It is impossible to find a person who cannot work in one place but can work in another place. This is not a question of knowledge. It is absolutely a question of whether or not one is a God-appointed gift. If you have the gift, others will be saved and helped through you, no matter how much knowledge you have. The amount of knowledge you have will not make any difference. What is a gift? A gift is an ability that God gives to the Body of Christ through Christ the Head. This ability does not change. I can illustrate this with an example. Suppose that there is a concrete worker in Shanghai. If he is in Nanking, he is still a concrete worker. Suppose that there is a tailor who is very skillful at sewing. Whether he is in Shanghai or Peking, he can still make a good dress. In the same way, circumstances will not change a gift.

But the same is not true with the eldership. The eldership is absolutely a question of locality. A person who is an elder in Shanghai is not an elder in Nanking. Because of differences in spiritual conditions, backgrounds, circumstances, educational standards, and the habits of different local assemblies, a man can be an elder in Shanghai but may no longer be able to serve as one in northern Kiangsu. A man may be an elder in the village, but not an elder in the city. This is absolutely a matter of locality. The gifts in the Bible are for the whole church, while the elders in the Bible are for the local churches. Therefore, those who have the gifts should not remain in one place all the time; they should instead go to other places and distribute their gifts to others. An elder should take responsibility in his own locality all the time. Consider the illustration of the concrete worker again. Suppose that you are a foreman among numerous concrete workers in Shanghai. If you move to Nanking, you will still be a concrete worker by profession, but you may not be able to be a foreman anymore. Doing concrete work is your ability, and your ability remains with you even after you have moved to Nanking. But the foremanship is a position; when you move to Nanking, your position as a foreman is gone. In the same way, there is a difference between office and gift in the Bible. An office and a position is for a local church, while a gift is not just for a local church. However, the mistake most easily committed is that when an elder in one locality moves to another locality, he asserts his own opinion there as well. This is wrong. Do not think that just because things are done one way in northern Kiangsu, it has to be done the same way in Shanghai. The educational standard and means of communication, etc., in northern Kiangsu may be different from those in Shanghai. You cannot use the same method in different places. However, gifts are different; if you are a gift in northern Kiangsu, you are one in Shanghai also.

QUESTIONS

Question: If we announce some unofficial elders among us, those in the denominations will say that we have become a denomination because we have brought in such a matter. How should we answer them?

Answer: First, let me ask what you have left behind when you leave the denominations. If you do not know what you have left behind, you will become another denomination. According to my personal understanding, when we leave the denominations, we leave two things behind: (1) We leave the divisive sects, such as the different denominations under the different names, and (2) the main thing we leave behind is the pastoral system. What is the pastoral system? It brings the intermediary priestly class of Judaism to Christianity. Both Catholicism and Protestantism have done this.

In the so-called Christian countries, Catholics have brought in the Judaistic teachings. In Judaism, there was the priestly class. The priests acted as an intermediary class. If a Jew wanted to see God, he had to pass through the hand of the priests; there was no way for him to go directly to God. The book of Judges records a certain man of Mount Ephraim by the name of Micah who made an ephod and invited a Levite to be the priest in his house (17:1-13). This is a clear example. What is Judaism? It is being kept away from worshipping God in a direct way. Between God and man, there was the need of priests to serve as an intermediary class. The Israelites had to go through the priests before they could see God. The same is true with Catholicism. God is on one side, and man is on the other side. There is no direct fellowship between them, and the priests serve as a medium in the middle. In the

Catholic Church, every time there is a mass, the priests are there. Every time there is any preaching, the priests are responsible for it, and every time there is prayer offered, the priests are the ones to do the work. In this way, men are brought back to the situation of the Old Testament.

Protestantism is divided into state churches and private churches. The Anglican Church in England serves as an example of the state churches. In the Anglican Church, there are the clergy and the laity. The bishops, archbishops, and deacons are all called priests, just as they are in Catholicism. This has likewise brought in Judaism. God is on the top, and the people, who are called the laity, are on the bottom. In the middle are the clergy, who call themselves priests. The laity can come to God only through this class of people, who monopolize all spiritual matters.

Among private churches in Protestantism (such as the Episcopal and Methodist), there is also the intermediary class. God is on the top, and the members are on the bottom. In between the two there are pastors. The pastors are the intermediary class, who replace the believers and monopolize all the spiritual matters that belong to the members. For example, administering the Holy Communion, baptism, and preaching are all done by pastors. They do everything for the members and become intermediaries between God and man. From Judaism until today, including all the denominations in Protestantism, God has always been on the top and man has been down on the bottom, with an intermediary class in between. Although the names may have changed, nothing has changed in substance.

Is this what we see in the New Testament? Peter said that we are a royal priesthood (1 Pet. 2:9). In Revelation, John also said that every Christian is a priest (1:6). Therefore, there is no need for any man to be a medium between us and God. In other words, we are all "pastors" and "priests." Hebrews 10 says that by the blood of Jesus, we have a new and living way to come boldly to the Holy of Holies (vv. 19-20). There is no need of an intermediary like the ones in Judaism, Catholicism, or Protestantism to help us draw near to God. Today we are not like the high priests in the Old Testament, who could go into the Holy of Holies only once a year. Daily, through the blood of the Lord, we can come to God. Every one of us is a priest, and every one can communicate with God boldly all the time. What then is Christianity? What is the new covenant? It is to annul the intermediary class. Every believer can now be directly responsible to God. Never consider the workers among us to be a kind of intermediary class like the ones in the private churches. There is no such thing. Every one of us can go to God. The workers do not occupy any position in the church; God is directly related to the church. Therefore, leaving the denominations is leaving two things behind: (1) the divisions, and (2) the pastoral system.

One Westerner once asked me why I am against pastors. I told him that I am not against pastors but rather the "pastoral system." If a man has the gift of a pastor, we cherish it. But whether or not a person has the gift of a pastor, we should not make him a priest and bring in a disguised priestly system. Even if one among us has the pastoral gift, we should not consider him as our priest or mediator.

I am afraid that in leaving the denominations some brothers consider that they are free from every control of man. They may think that since they have left the denominations, they can be lawless and free, doing anything they want. If this is the way you are, I have to call you by another name: you have not left the denominations; you have left the church. You are not freeing yourself from the denominations but from authority. We have left the denominations in order to leave the divisions and pastoral system. The purpose is not that we would become individual, isolated believers. Rather, we have the God-ordained authority with us. Therefore, submitting to man is submitting to God's authority, and submitting to the brothers is submitting to God's authority.

The Gospel of Luke records the Lord Jesus as saying, "Did you not know that I must be in the things of My Father?" (2:49). He had to be in the things of the Father but, at the same time, He went back home with His parents. This is the submission of the Lord Jesus. If it were us, we would not have done this. If we had said that we had to be in the things of our Father, we would not have returned with our parents.

However, this would only have been a proof of our disobedience. Being in the things of the Father includes being under the authority of the Father, which also includes submitting to God's authority in the parents. Therefore, when we submit to men, we are submitting to authority. Do not think that by leaving the denominations, we can become free and lawless and that no one can rule over us. If we think this way, we are more evil than the most evil persons in the world, and we become worse than those who have not left the denominations, because those who have not left the denominations are still under man's authority even though they do not have the God-ordained authority. But we do not even submit to God's authority. The Bible does not have denominations, but it has elders. We are giving up the denominations, which are not found in the Bible; we are not giving up the elders, which are found in the Bible. Just because the denominations have elders, we should not say that we can give up the scripturally-based eldership because we have left the denominations. There are brothers in the denominations; we cannot say that we are giving up the brothers just because we have given up the denominations.

Question: Are the elders appointed by God?

Answer: Acts 20 clearly says that the Holy Spirit has placed men to be overseers over the flock. Therefore, elders are appointed by God. What the apostles did merely expressed the intention of the Holy Spirit.

Question: How should the elders be supported? Is the support for the elders the same as the support for the workers?

Answer: There is no difference between the two. In the Bible, there is no such thing as a worker giving up his salary and becoming a special supported class. Although Peter gave up his fishing, Paul remained a tentmaker. There is no difference between a worker with an occupation and a worker without an occupation; there is no distinction of class. If an elder is gifted and is so busy with the affairs of the church that he has no more time to take up an occupation, he should receive double honor from the brothers. If an elder is not that busy, he can hold a job to support himself and also take care of the church affairs. This is true not only with the elders but with the workers as well. Those who are gifted can hold a job, and they can also do their work, as long as their job does not interfere with their work. I also hope that I can do my work while holding a job. I am not saying this because I am poor and have nothing to eat. Living by faith is not something that makes one holier than others. Yet some consider this to be something extraordinary and super-spiritual. The reason Christians pay too much attention to those who live by faith is that the faith of Christians has become degraded. Actually, there is nothing strange about this matter. The very early churches did not consider this to be something strange. Actually, every believer should have faith, and every person who is holding a job should live by faith. I have often thought that those brothers who are engaged in business have a greater faith than I have. If they do not have faith, how can they open a shop, put in capital, and order the merchandise? How do they know if people will buy the merchandise?

In the Bible the elders are brothers, the gifted ones are brothers, and those who do not have any gift are brothers also. Among the brothers, there are only distinctions between gifts and positions; there is no distinction between having and not having a job. Such a distinction in support is a concept brought in from the denominations. Those who hold such a concept have forgotten that Paul was a tentmaker. For this reason, we should completely eradicate this concept from among us. If a pastor in a denomination, on the one hand, serves as a pastor and, on the other hand, holds a job, others will misunderstand him. But among us, we should not have such a concept. This kind of concept is a poison left behind by the pastoral system of the denominations.

The Catholic Church says that after a man is ordained, he becomes holy. He will have an indelible mark on him, and it will distinguish him from other, common people. But Catholicism has forgotten that the apostle Paul continued to hold a job of making tents. We workers can give up our job when we are busy and go back to our jobs when we have time. There is nothing wrong in doing this.

Question: Can an evangelist start a school by himself?

Answer: Yes, he can. A person can start a business or a

school by himself. Paul might have started a business of tent-making. But he did not involve all the believers in Ephesus in this tentmaking business.

It is wrong for a church to run a school, hospital, or biscuit factory. It is all right for some brothers to join together to start a school, hospital, or biscuit factory. But it is a big mistake if we run a school under the name of the meeting in Hardoon Road. It is not wrong for a few brothers to start a school together.

Question: Is it true that in the whole Bible, pastors are mentioned only in Ephesians 4?

Answer: Yes, this is true. The word *pastor* or *shepherd* (as related to the church) is mentioned only in Ephesians 4. [Editor's note: This is according to the Chinese Union Version Bible.] Pastoring or shepherding is a gift and is for the building up of the whole church; it is a gift that God has given to the whole church. The elders, on the other hand, are appointed by the apostles for the purpose of managing a local church (known as the so-called congregation in the denominations). Yet the apostles cannot appoint gifts; they have never appointed any prophets, evangelists, or shepherds and teachers, because these are gifts given by God. Suppose I am the owner of a factory. I can appoint foremen and assistant foremen because these are positions. But I cannot appoint anyone to be a concrete worker, because a person may not know how to do concrete work. Therefore, an apostle can only appoint men to offices, that is, to the eldership; he cannot appoint gifts, such as prophets, evangelists, or shepherds and teachers, because the matter of gifts is entirely in God's hand. God appoints them, and God gives these gifts. No one can usurp or fight for them. If you see someone who is good at preaching, and you want to be the same, it cannot be done. This is because 1 Corinthians 12 says that gifts are not appointed by men and are not obtained according to human will; they are distributed to all respectively even as He purposes (v. 11). Pastoring is a gift of the Holy Spirit and is given to the church by God through the Spirit. If we see anyone with the gift of pastoring, we cherish it. But we cannot ordain a man to be a pastor, just as we cannot ordain a man to be a concrete worker. We must not force the pastors to become priests, the intermediary class. If anyone does this, we will surely oppose it. But this does not mean that we are opposed to the pastors or shepherds that are recorded in the Bible. We are opposed to the "pastoral system" that is in the denominations. This is why we have to be careful not to bring the things invented by the denominations into our midst.

Question: Can elders be elected by the believers?

Answer: No. Elders cannot be elected, because they are appointed by the apostles. Presently, they are appointed by those who are doing the work of the apostles. The Bible never uses the method of election. Only once in Acts is the word *appoint* used; it is used in the appointment of the first seven deacons (6:3). Actually, these deacons were first tested by the apostles and then appointed.

Question: There are so many pastors in the denominations. Can it be possible that not one of them is a genuine pastor?

Answer: As far as their ordination is concerned, no human-ordained pastor is a pastor. As far as their gifts are concerned, it is possible that among those who are ordained by men, some have the gift of pastoring. No one can become a pastor through human examination, graduation from seminaries, ordination, or invitation. There has never been such a pastor in history. If he is truly a pastor, he must have received the gift of pastoring from God.

Question: How does the pastoral gift build the church?

Answer: The word *pastor* has been used only once in Ephesians 4 [according to the Chinese Union Version Bible]. In other passages, the word is translated "shepherd." The words *pastor* and *shepherd* are the same word in the original language. The meaning of this word is to feed and guard. Those who are given the gift of pastoring should be able to lead and feed the believers. They should be able to lead others to grow step by step, discuss and study the Bible with others, and pray with others.

An evangelist is one who leads others to salvation and brings in men. A teacher is one who can release the truth and make others understand and see the truth in a clear way.

A pastor or shepherd is one who leads others to advance; he does not necessarily have to be able to preach, though some are indeed able to preach. The function of the pastors is to feed the believers.

Question: Can a woman have the pastoral gift?

Answer: Gifts are given without distinction of sex. A woman can also have the pastoral gift. The daughters of Philip had the gift of prophecy.

Question: Can sisters testify and preach the gospel to unbelieving men?

Answer: The Bible has not clearly said no to this, but neither has the Bible encouraged it. There is no clear pattern in the Bible for us to follow. Personally, I think that if the sisters do anything beyond their covered position, they have gone beyond their limit. The covering that I am speaking of does not refer only to a piece of cloth on the head (which is also an important sign) but to the hidden and submissive position which God has allotted them. Even brothers should have their heads covered before God. The brothers cover their head under Christ. Christ is the head of everyone, while the man is the head of the woman (1 Cor. 11:3). Therefore, a woman has two heads. On the one hand, a woman covers her head in Christ and, on the other hand, she covers her head through the man. The covering on a woman's head symbolizes her submission under the authority of the brothers and her not acting in an independent way. The sisters can do many good and precious things. But they have to take a few brothers as their covering so that both glory and shame will fall on these brothers. Therefore, it is improper for sisters to go to a place to do some pioneering work alone.

A certain Western magazine once reported the words of a sister: "I used to think that I had to do everything by myself and that I had to charge forward alone. When I became sick and returned to my home country, I discovered that everything I had done was wrong, and I confessed my mistakes to God." Many people think that since Deborah was raised up from the Israelites, there could be one today. But we have to remember that not every Israelite woman was a Deborah! Moreover, even Deborah took Barak as her head. All genuine women want to do this. All genuine women honor what God has done, and they honor the place and order that God has placed them in. Because I am not a sister, it is somewhat difficult for me to say these words. If I were a sister, I would be more free to say this. Sisters should always stand in a covered position. This does not mean that sisters should not work. It merely means that God has appointed the brothers to be the protector of the sisters. The ones who assume the headship should be the brothers; all the glory and shame should go to the brothers. This does not mean that the brothers covet the sisters' glory. Rather it means that the brothers protect the sisters and maintain the order God has established.

It is a woman's nature to stand in a non-prominent position. This is why Paul reminded the women that their nature tells them this. If a wife sits in the place of a husband and becomes the husband's head in a family, how can that family stand? It will surely not stand. If a church acts this way, will it still be a church? The virtuous woman recorded in Proverbs labors, works, and hopes that her husband receives the glory in the gate of the city.

The most precious thing is to be submissive to authority. The relationship between a servant and his master, a child and his parents, a wife and her husband, a citizen and his country, and a woman and a man should be one of submission to authority. God pays much attention to the question of authority, while Satan pays much attention to power. If a man only asks if a thing can be done and does not ask if a thing should be done, he has fallen already. Therefore, every sister should stand in the position of submission to God's authority. The question of authority is the greatest and most crucial one. Unfortunately, it has produced little effect on the brothers and sisters.

Therefore, according to the light of the Bible, sisters should not open their mouth in the church meetings. If they want to testify or preach the gospel to individual men or to groups of men, they should do it in a covered position.

Question: Can one person possess two gifts?

Answer: Yes, he can. Sometimes a person can even possess three gifts.

Question: Was Peter the first pastor?

Answer: We can say that.

Question: Why did we not mention the matter concerning the elders earlier or even later than now? Why do we have to mention it now and stir up misunderstandings that we have become a denomination by having elders?

Answer: The question of elders was mentioned two to three years ago. At that time, no one was raised up who resembled an elder. That was merely a transitional period. The Bible says that a novice should not be an elder. There must be a transitional period. Now the time has come, and we can bring up the matter of the elders. If we go on without any elders raised up among us, we will become a lawless body.

Question: Among us, we may have men who resemble the elders, but they do not have the official title of an elder. This is like having no official title of apostles at the present time. Is this right?

Answer: This is right. If someone asks you what we are and whether or not we are the church in Shanghai, how should you answer? You should say that we are not the church in Shanghai. If someone asks if we are the church on Hardoon Road, you should say no. We should not admit that we are the church in Shanghai, because besides us there are the Shou-jin Chapel, the Mu-re Chapel, the Chin-lin Chapel, etc. There are many saved ones who are not meeting with us. We do not admit that we are the church on Hardoon Road either, because there may be many people who live on Hardoon Road who are not meeting with us. If we call ourselves the church in Shanghai, we have to include all believers in Shanghai. Otherwise, we cannot be considered the church in Shanghai.

They may then ask you what you are if you are not the church. We admit that we are not the church; we are merely those who meet on the ground of the church. I can illustrate the point by an example. The temple in the Old Testament was built in a splendid way. Later, it was burned, and not one stone was left on top of another. Suppose a man in Jerusalem at that time decided to erect a tent on the foundation of the burnt temple. If others were to ask him what this was, he would say that it was not the temple: rather, it was only a tent on the ground of the temple. The same is true with our meeting today. If others ask us what we are, we have to answer that we are not the church; we are not the church in Shanghai. We are a group of brothers and sisters in Shanghai meeting on the ground of the church. We are those who meet according to the principle of the church as revealed in the Bible. We are those who intend to stand on the ground of the church to maintain the ground of the church. The temple is now in ruins and burned, and we are only a tent. All those who have eyes can see the degradation of the church today; outwardly, everything is in ruins. We cannot and dare not call ourselves the church in Shanghai. We only desire to meet on the ground of the church based on the light we have received concerning the church. We are not the church in Shanghai, but we are meeting in a way that maintains and upholds the church in Shanghai. We are standing on the same ground that the church stands on, yet we are not the very church itself. Therefore, even though we are not the temple, we are a miniature of the temple, and we are here to express the life of the temple. This is why the elders and deacons among us are non-official. The reason we have elders and deacons is that, even though we admit that we are a small tent, we are, nevertheless, erected on the ground of the temple. Therefore, we have to do everything according to the pattern of the temple.

At the time of the Babylonians, the temple was destroyed. After Nehemiah and Ezra returned from their exile and rebuilt the temple, the old men who had seen the glory of the first temple knew that the rebuilt temple could not match the first one. But men like Nehemiah and Ezra still offered sacrifices according to the former principle of offerings even though the temple was no longer the same as the first temple.

The temple mentioned in John 2 was not the first temple; it was merely a rebuilt temple. Yet the Lord Jesus drove out the cattle and sheep from that temple and said that it was "My Father's house" (v. 16). The Lord said that because He was standing on the ground of the temple. Although the temple was no longer the same as the first one, the ground of the temple was the same, and the principles of the temple remained. Although the outward structure may collapse, the ground remains, and upon this ground, there is still the possibility of maintaining the principle of service to God on a small scale.

There were twelve tribes in the nation of Israel. Yet God established Jerusalem as the place He chose to put His name. All the tribes had to come to Jerusalem three times a year to offer sacrifices and worship God. Later when Rehoboam was king, the nation was divided into Judah and Israel. The nation of Judah had two tribes and continued to worship God in Jerusalem. The nation of Israel had ten tribes, and Jeroboam was their king. Nevertheless, they obeyed God's command to go to Jerusalem three times a year to worship Him. However, Jeroboam was afraid that journeying to Jerusalem three times a year would turn the people's heart to the king of Judah, causing them to rebel against him and leave him. Therefore, he set up an altar in Bethel—the place which men considered the best—made a golden calf, and charged the people to worship there instead of going to Jerusalem to worship. At that time, a young prophet rebuked him, prophesied, and gave a sign by putting forth his hand to the altar. When Jeroboam heard the word of the prophet, he put forth his hand and tried to lay hold of the prophet, but his hand dried up, and he could not pull it in again to him (1 Kings 13:3-4). In the end, he had to allow the people to return to Jerusalem. From this we see that *although the people were divided outwardly, the principle of service to God should not be lost.* The human Bethel can never replace God's Jerusalem. The outward law cannot replace God's ordination. No political division can change God's principle. Therefore, no outward destruction, failure, or desolation can ever change God's ordained principles.

When the Israelites divided the land, nine and a half tribes remained on the west side of the Jordan in the land promised by God, while two and a half tribes preferred to dwell on the east side of the Jordan. Under the hand of Joshua, the two and a half tribes finished the division of the land. Then they

erected a great altar by the river Jordan. When the whole congregation of Israel heard this, they went up to attack the two
and a half tribes because they thought the two and a half
tribes were trying "to build an altar...besides the altar of the
Lord our God" (Josh. 22:29). Not only is it a sin to turn away
from following Jehovah, it is a sin even to offer the burnt
offering, meal offering, and peace offering on an altar other
than the altar of the Lord. The two and a half tribes answered
that they had no intention of erecting another center of worship, and that they were not erecting a new altar but were
merely making a testimony. Only the altar before the taber-
nacle of God is the proper place of worship (Josh. 22). The two
and a half tribes represent those who have failed spiritually.
But the ones who have failed cannot change the principle of
worship that God has ordained. Although, after the separation, Israel was no longer one nation outwardly and no longer
the original kingdom of David, all of the Israelites still had to
worship in Jerusalem. Therefore, although there is division
and failure in Shanghai, although there is division and failure in the churches everywhere, and although there is
desolation outwardly, we still have to worship God by standing on the ground of the church. This is a matter of principle.
This is also the reason for us to appoint the elders. This is
why we have elders among us today, but these elders are not
official ones. We do not have elders like those in the denominations.

Question: Will God take back the gifts at times?

Answer: The gifts are given by God, and God never takes
back the gifts. We can have three different attitudes toward
God's gifts: (1) we can misuse them, like the Corinthians;
(2) we can bury them, like the one in Matthew 25; and (3) God
can stop the gifts. Through man's unbelief, some gifts such as
the gift of prophecy become no longer available.

Question: Can we ask for the gifts?

Answer: Yes. First Corinthians 14 clearly says that we
should pursue the gifts.

Question: What does it mean to misuse the gifts?

Answer: God does not take back the gifts. At the time of
judgment, God will ask us how we have used our gifts. If a

man misuses his gifts, he is using them according to his human way or for his own glory, as the Corinthians did. Yet God does not take back the gifts, because the gifts and calling of God are irrevocable (Rom. 11:29). Suppose a sister preaches the gospel in a meeting, and a man is saved. One may ask that since a sister should not preach to a man, why is she able to lead a man to salvation? I can tell you that this is indeed an exercise of the gift, but it is a misuse of the gift. It is God's gift that is saving men. Sometimes, a gospel preacher goes to a wrong place to preach the gospel and saves a few men. Yet this also is a misuse of the gift. Those who bury their gifts are usually those who have only one talent. The more they consider that their gifts are insignificant, the less they exercise them. The gifts stop because the believers do not have the faith to use them.

Question: Can a man know whether or not he has a gift?

Answer: Sometimes he can and sometimes he cannot, but others know. In most cases, others know through the fruit of his work. The Corinthians knew in themselves that they had the gifts. Some feel sorry for Moses because he did not know the glory that was shining on his own face. Yet it was fortunate that Moses did not know, for had he known that his face was shining, the shining would have gone away. Therefore, we should allow others to find out if we have the gifts.

Question: If misusing or burying the gifts will bring God's judgment, is it better that we do not ask for the gifts lest we fall into judgment?

Answer: The more gift a believer has, the more chance there is for him to receive the reward. The more reward a believer has, the more glory he will receive. If a believer has never been dealt with, it is better that he does not ask for gifts lest he fail in the future judgment. But those who know God should ask for more gifts, so that they can use them for the church and not for themselves. I do hope that God will raise up more gifted ones.

Question: How do we know that we are misusing the gifts?

Answer: In the parable of the talents in Matthew 25, there are three kinds of gifts—five talents, two talents, and one talent. They were given to three slaves, who were told to do business. The gifts are the capital. When the slaves took the gifts to do business, they could make a profit or incur a loss. If they made a profit, their master would not suffer. If they incurred a loss, their master would suffer. Brothers who have the gift of evangelism can surely save people. But if their works are not done according to God's will and if they are doing these for self-glorification, to meet some personal needs, or for the sake of going along with human affections, they will lose their spiritual power and will be left only with the power of their gifts. Today, many of God's servants are leading conferences, reviving men, helping men, and saving men. Among them, some are indeed gifts given by God. You may find out that although they have the gifts, they do not want to stand on the ground that God wants them to stand on. You may be amazed that they can still save, help, and revive men when they themselves are not standing on the ground God wants them to stand on. Actually, this is a misuse of the gifts. They can save and revive men because they have God's gifts. It is God's gifts that are saving men, reviving men, and helping men. This kind of misuse of gifts is very dangerous. Today God does not interfere and does not say anything. But when we go before the judgment seat, He will reckon with us. As in the parable mentioned in Matthew 25, He will reckon with us according to the amount of gifts that He gave us as capital and according to the way we did business in the world with these gifts.

We must never think that, as long as we have a fine and thriving work and others love to listen to us, we are right. We have to beware of misusing our gifts. Many times, it is possible for a believer to preach out of a desire for fame and praise from man. But the conscience knows that this is wrong. Once a brother went to a place to preach the gospel. When he returned, I asked about his work. He told me that he went and came back, and a few persons were saved. Yet he still did not know if it was God's will for him to go. This is to misuse the gift. God has entrusted the gifts in your hand, and He will not reckon with you until the time of the judgment seat. Yet we should consider God to be reckoning with us every day. If we think that He will not reckon with us until many years afterward, we may use our gifts in a careless way.

A gift is a kind of spiritual ability, capacity, power, and knowledge which enables one to work. For example, I may be very good at calligraphy. Whether or not I have a proper fellowship with God, my calligraphy remains good. If I am in God's will, I write good calligraphy; if I am not in God's will, I still write good calligraphy. The same is true with the gifts. When we are in God's will, we can help others when we exercise our gift. When we are not in God's will, we can still help others when we exercise our gift. (Of course, there is a question of whether or not such help indeed has any spiritual value to it.) But we will reckon with the sin of misusing our gifts when we face the judgment seat. This is why we have to be careful that we do not work for glory, praise, men's approval, fame, profit, or to gratify ourselves. If we do, we are misusing the gift.

Question: Does every believer have a gift?

Answer: Yes. Every believer has at least one talent. There is no slave who does not have any gift. First Corinthians 12 says that to one is given one kind of gift and to another is given another kind of gift. Therefore, everyone has some gift. Every regenerated person has a gift. But not everyone has the same kind of gift. According to Ephesians 4, there are only five kinds of gifts that build up the whole church. But as to the gifts that are for the growth of a local church, we have those mentioned in 1 Corinthians 12 and Romans 12. Not every believer has the gifts of Ephesians 4, but they may have one of the gifts mentioned in Romans 12 and 1 Corinthians 12.

Question: How can we know that we are not misusing the gifts?

Answer: In order not to misuse the gifts, we have to accept the cross of Christ. The cross of Christ, the flesh-severing cross, is the basis of everything. The reason there are problems in all the local assemblies and in the church is that the brothers and sisters are not willing to accept the cross of Christ. Everything that issues from the resurrection of Christ is for the Body of Christ; every problem in the church arises when men try to drag out things that belong in the grave. If we are willing to accept Christ's cross and are willing to allow it to do a deeper work in us, removing our ambitions and grand aspirations, we will not misuse our gifts. For example, yesterday I mentioned the matter of the elders. Who are the ones who are not qualified to be elders? They are those who, upon hearing about the matter related to an elder, expect to be an elder themselves. Who are the ones who are qualified to be elders? They are those who, upon hearing about the matter related to an elder, consider themselves unworthy to be one. Those who aspire to be the authority are not qualified to be the authority; authority can never be placed in their hand. Only those who do not aspire to be the authority are qualified to be the authority.

Question: Why does 1 Timothy 3 say that one has to aspire to be an elder?

Answer: It is because many people may withdraw. Today there are many people who are like Peter, who refuse to be washed. Both fleshly boasting and fleshly withdrawal are of the flesh and are two sides of one truth. First Timothy 3 says that a novice should not be an overseer lest he become proud and fall into the snare of the devil. The Lord is telling these ones not to aspire to be an elder lest they fall into the devil's snare through their pride. But to those who consider themselves useless, who realize the weakness of their flesh, who consider themselves unworthy, and who are withdrawn, the Lord encourages them by telling them that overseership is a good work and is to be desired. God tells those who volunteer to be elders that they are not worthy and encourages those who are worthy but withdrawn to be elders. May all the brothers see that there are two sides to the flesh; either it boasts of itself or it withdraws. We must never consider the boasting of the flesh as a kind of courage and the withdrawing of the flesh as a kind of humility. When we consider our own virtues, we become proud; when we consider our own weaknesses and failures, we dare not do anything and withdraw. We should not confuse boasting with courage and withdrawal with humility. Actually, real humility is not considering one's own goodness or weakness. This is why someone has said that real humility is not considering oneself. Boldness is being strengthened in the Lord and looking at the Lord only. This is why Ephesians 6 says that we have to be empowered in the Lord. All those who carefully weigh themselves and become confident in themselves are boastful; they are not bold. On the one hand, we must look to the Lord and, on the other hand, not look to ourselves. In this way, we will be bold as well as humble. This is victory. Many fail because they look at either the powerful side of the flesh or the weak side of the flesh. As a result, they become either a person who boasts in the flesh or a person who withdraws in the flesh. The above discussion touches a principle. This principle can be applied not only to the appointment of the elders and the deacons but to other daily affairs as well.

Question: Do the apostles, prophets, evangelists, shepherds, and teachers in Ephesians 4 refer to people or do they refer to things or titles?

Answer: Ephesians 4 refers to people, while 1 Corinthians 12 refers to things. Ephesians 4 says that God gives some apostles, prophets, evangelists, and shepherds and teachers; these are five kinds of people. First Corinthians 12 says that God gives some the ability to prophesy or speak in tongues. Paul was a gift given by God to the church; he was an apostle. But Paul also had other gifts, such as prophesying, speaking in tongues, and healing.

To my observation, Brother Chi Yung-tung looks very much like a pastor. Let me take him as an example. God has given a gift to the church in Soo-chia-tsui, which is Chi Yung-tung. The whole church in Soo-chia-tsui should then receive Brother Chi as a gift given to them by God. At the same time, Brother Chi has the pastoral gift. His gift is the gift of a pastor. If anyone asks what gift Paul had, we would answer that he had the gift of an apostle. But if anyone asks what gift God has given to the church, we would answer, "The apostle Paul." All five kinds of people in Ephesians 4 are gifts given by God to the church, and they are for the whole church. First Corinthians 12 mentions the various gifts that God gives to individual believers; the gifts in 1 Corinthians 12 are for the local churches. Paul was a gift given by God to the whole church. Ephesians 4 mentions men as gifts given by God to the church for the purpose of building up the whole church. Therefore, the gift which was released through Paul has benefited men of all times and places; his work did not pass away; it remains even until today.

Question: How do we deal with lawless brothers in the meetings?

Answer: If a man continually disturbs the meeting but does not have obvious sins that deserve excommunication, we should deal with him in a severe way according to the teaching of Romans 16:17. We should mark him and not communicate with him. "Now I exhort you, brothers, to mark those who make divisions and causes of stumbling contrary to the teaching which you have learned, and turn away from them." We should not place the affairs of the church in the hands of these ones. Whatever the church is doing, these ones should be excluded from it.

Question: How should one deal with an elder who is involved with some problems?

Answer: The eldership in the Bible is plural in number. If one elder is involved with some problems, the other elders should deal with him.

Question: If the elders are unofficial, does this mean that we can accuse them only in an unofficial way?

Answer: That is right. If one elder is wrong, the other elders can deal with him. This is why the Bible never uses the word *elder* in a singular sense; it is always *elders,* plural. Therefore, this does not present too much of a problem.

DEACONS

Deacons are the serving ones in the Bible. In the church there should not only be responsible ones like the elders, but the church should also have serving ones like the deacons. The church needs men who give proposals and who manage and oversee the brothers, like the elders. The church also needs dedicated serving ones to take care of all the miscellaneous affairs, like the deacons. The ones who make decisions, manage the church, make proposals, oversee, and observe from top to bottom are the elders. The ones who execute the affairs, run errands, take orders, and help others in being directed are the deacons. God needs the elders to be the doorkeepers, and He needs the deacons to work and run errands for the believers. For example, the money of an assembly is kept by the deacons, while the authority to use the money is with the elders. All matters related to the brothers are directed and decided by the elders and announced by the deacons. The elders are the foremen, and the deacons are the workmen. The deacons do not have any proposals of their own; they only work according to the direction of the elders. The deacons are those who help the elders accomplish things. (Concerning the deacons, much is recorded in the books of Timothy and Titus.) I hope that some brothers among us would be raised up to be the deacons, and I hope that some sisters among us would also be raised up to be the deaconesses. The Bible records deaconesses. The deacons and deaconesses are dedicated to the handling and management of affairs.

QUESTIONS

Question: Is the selection of the deacons by way of voting?

Answer: No. During the early years, there were not many scrolls with which to write everything down. The selection of deacons in the time of the apostles was not by a vote of the majority. The deacons were first approved by the apostles and manifested to be deacons in a most natural way. The scriptural way of selecting the deacons is to allow the deacons to become manifest in a natural way. Those who were qualified to be deacons were selected by the church and acknowledged by the apostles. We should practice the same today.

Question: Why was the selection of Matthias by the way of casting lots?

Answer: The Holy Spirit had not yet descended, and the disciples did not know which one should fill the place. They selected two and decided which one of the two should fill up the apostleship.

Question: Does not Acts 6 say that the disciples appointed seven deacons?

Answer: Acts 6 does not say explicitly that these seven

were the deacons. It only shows us that they were doing the work of deacons. Therefore, we can only say that they were the deacons by the things they did. When Acts mentions Philip, it says that he was one of the seven; it does not say that he was one of the seven deacons. Therefore, although there are deacons in the Bible, it does not say clearly that the deacons are elected. I think that the matter of selection of the deacons should be treated in the same way as the appointment of the elders, that is, they should be appointed by the apostles and sent by the apostles. We should be careful not to investigate what the Bible has purposely left blank and unexplained.

Question: When should elders and deacons be appointed?

Answer: The sooner they are appointed, the better.

Question: If a local meeting has only three brothers, who should be the elders and deacons?

Answer: The only thing that can be done is for these few brothers to function as elders and deacons at the same time. In the whole Bible, only the book of Philippians gives a complete description of the church, which includes the saints, the elders, and the deacons. It tells us that the church is composed of the saints, elders, and deacons: "Paul and Timothy, slaves of Christ Jesus, to all the saints in Christ Jesus who are in Philippi, with the overseers and deacons" (Phil. 1:1).

Question: Why does 1 Timothy say that a man must be approved before he can be appointed a deacon?

Answer: The deacons are those who are dedicated to handling affairs. The deacons are always the younger ones. They may act in the flesh. Therefore, they must first be tested a few times. They must first be sent to handle affairs a few times, before one can decide if they are qualified to be a deacon.

Question: If a few brothers begin to meet in a place, what should they have first, deacons or elders?

Answer: They should first have responsible ones and then the bread-breaking meeting. They should first have elders and then deacons. This is the teaching in Acts. Antioch is one example. There should at least be one brother who can take responsibility before the bread-breaking meeting is initiated. Otherwise, the bread-breaking meeting will not be proper. Moreover, from the beginning there should be the teaching of submission to the elders and the teaching of submission one to another when the meeting starts. Otherwise, in a meeting of five people, the five will become five big denominations. When this happens, these five may still remember the Lord at the bread-breaking meeting, but they will not be able to discern the Body; they will not consider themselves the Body of Christ. They will care only for themselves and take only themselves as the head. Therefore, we should learn to submit to the elders and also learn to submit to one another.

CHAPTER TWO

THE PRACTICE OF FELLOWSHIP

THERE BEING ONLY ONE CHURCH

The Bible says that there is only one church. The church which Paul was in is the same church that we are in. The church that we are in is the same church that the apostle John, Martin Luther, John Calvin, and all regenerated persons are in. The church in the Bible is not separated by time, locality, or race. There is only one church, which exists at all times and in all places. There are not two churches. The Bible only recognizes one Body of Christ and never recognizes two, because there is only one Head. Although there are many members in the Bible, the Body is singular. Therefore, all saved persons past and present, here and elsewhere constitute one church and one Body. If this is the case, why are there "churches" in different places? Since Ephesians mentions one Body, one Spirit, one hope, one Lord, one faith, one baptism, and one God, why does the Bible mention churches also? Is this not a contradiction? Why is it that, on the one hand, there is only one Body, but on the other hand, there are many churches? This shows us that there are different views in the Bible concerning the Body of Christ and the local churches. Strictly speaking, there is only one church, in the same way that there is only one Body of Christ. However, in each locality, there may be as many as three to five thousand believers, or there may be as few as two or three, as described in Matthew 18. As long as there is a group of believers meeting together in a city or a town, that group of believers constitutes the church in that city or town. Therefore, in the original language, the Bible clearly shows us that the church is "the church in such-and-such place." The word *in* indicates that there is only one church, which is scattered and sojourning in different places. The Bible calls the meeting of those who sojourn and meet together in one place a local church; it serves as a miniature representation of the unique church.

We treasure very much the words in Romans 12 which say, "We who are many are one Body." "We" includes all the believers. There is only one bread. Therefore, do not think that we have one bread in Wen-teh Lane and another bread in Gordon Lane, and yet another in Peking or Changchun. Materially speaking, in the whole world there can be hundreds and thousands of loaves, but before God there is only one bread, spiritually speaking. However, we cannot participate in only one bread, because we are limited in our flesh by time and space. If it were possible, all the believers in the world would break only one bread. Although brothers can break bread in Changchun, Peking, Hangchow, or Nan-shu-chow, there is only one bread before God. The one bread that we touch on the Lord's Day evening in Shanghai is the same bread that Brother Luan touched in Hangchow and that Brother Hwang touched in Nan-shu-chow. The bread that is broken in every place and the Body of Christ that it represents is the same bread and same Body of Christ in every place. God has only one church in the world. This one church is scattered *in* all the cities and villages. These scattered churches in the cities and villages are called the churches in those cities or the churches in those villages. For convenience' sake, we call the churches in all the cities and villages the churches of God. Actually, the churches of God are just the church of God. The Lord charges us to break the bread every Lord's Day in order to remind us that the churches in the various localities are not independent churches but are joined as one church. This is why we have the symbol of the one bread. The one bread reminds us that although there are many believers in all places and at all times, and although there are many local churches, we are still one bread.

I do not like to use political figures for illustration, because the subject of politics is too fashionable. But I have to use one today. The Nationalist Party of China respects Mr. Sun Yat-sen to the utmost. All government offices have the picture of Mr. Sun. There may be thousands and tens of thousands of pictures of Mr. Sun, but the person they represent is the same. In the same way, we may be breaking thousands of loaves of bread, but the Body of Christ, which these loaves represent, is just one, and the Lord, whom these loaves represent, is just one. Therefore, the miniature churches in all the places are representations of the whole Body of Christ. When we see a local assembly with fifty people meeting, we should realize immediately that they represent all the believers at all times and in all places. Today in Gordon Lane there are over fifty people meeting. If in Bao-shan there are only seven or eight people meeting, the bread which they break before the Lord at the Lord's table includes Peter, Paul, Martin Luther, Wesley, and others; it also includes you and me. Therefore, whether it be the meeting in Bao-shan, Hangchow, Soo-chia-tsui, or anywhere else, all these meetings represent the Body of Christ. This is why no church can act independently. All the moves must take care of the whole church. While you are sitting in a meeting, you should not see only the brothers and sisters next to you but the whole Body of Christ. What you are doing affects not only the one or two hundred people who are meeting with you; it affects the whole Body of Christ because we only have one Body. Although you are only a member, what you do is what the Body of Christ does. One member can drag down the whole Body.

Most of the Chinese who live in Southeast Asia are from the provinces of Fukien and Kwangtung. Everywhere in Southeast Asia, whether in a village or in a city, one can find Chinese Associations. The number of members in these associations may vary, but if an association receives respect in one place, it means that the whole Chinese race receives respect in that place, and if an association is persecuted in a place, it means that the whole Chinese race is persecuted in that place. Just as these associations represent China in Southeast Asia, we represent the church in our respective localities. Since this is the case, we can see how intimately related the conduct of an individual church is to the conduct of the Body of Christ. We can also see the relationship between the various assemblies. Although you are a miniature church and a small community within a certain boundary, God intends that this miniature church, this small community, express the large-scale church, the large community. Therefore, what we are doing in the small local churches represents and includes all that the Body of Christ does. For this reason, we have to be related to other local churches and the brothers and sisters in the other localities.

RECEIVING A PERSON
INTO THE BREAD-BREAKING MEETING

If a brother has been received into the bread-breaking meeting, he is not received into the assembly in Hangchow, Tientsin, or Soo-chow but into the churches of God, the (outward) house of God. When we receive a brother in Hangchow, we are receiving him on behalf of the churches in Tientsin, Shanghai, Soo-chow, and other places. If we intend to receive a person in Shanghai and think that the brothers in Hangchow and Peking may not receive him, we should not receive him either. We cannot act independently. If you know that the thing you are about to do in your locality will be considered inappropriate in other localities, you must not take care of the views of the few in your locality and do it anyway. If you do it, you are not discerning the Body of Christ. If what we do individually cannot represent the brothers in Shanghai, we should not do it. By the same token, if a matter cannot pass the unanimous approval of the whole church, it is not a move of the Body but an individual move. In the Bible there is only the move of the Body; there is no move of individuals.

If a brother wants to be received into the bread-breaking meeting, we must examine him carefully because we are receiving him not only on behalf of the brothers in Shanghai, but also on behalf of the brothers meeting in Tientsin, Hangchow, Wenchow, and other places. However, when a brother goes to another locality to break bread, the brothers in the locality should not examine him further. All he needs to do is to bring a letter of recommendation with him. The brothers in the other localities should believe what the brothers in Shanghai have done and receive him into the bread-breaking meeting based on the letter of recommendation. We have to be very careful in what we do in order to care for the brothers in the other localities.

RECOGNITION OF THE GIFTS

Furthermore, if the brothers meeting in Soo-chia-tsui in northern Kiangsu recognize a certain person as having a certain gift, whether a pastor, teacher, or evangelist, he should be able to be a pastor, teacher, or evangelist in Shanghai as well. The brothers in Shanghai should recognize the gift of such a person also. A gifted person does not lose his gift by moving from one locality to another locality. Therefore, a local assembly has to recognize the gifts that are recognized by another local assembly. If God has given a person the pastoral gift, he will be recognized as a pastor in northern Kiangsu, and we should also recognize his pastoral gift when he comes into our midst. If Shanghai recognizes a certain person as having the ability to preach the gospel, Peking should recognize the same thing. Although offices may change through change of location, gifts do not change through moving to a different location. Gifts are not local, but offices are local. Therefore, every time an assembly wants to recognize a gift, it has to be careful because not only does that particular assembly have to recognize his gift, but the brothers in other places have to recognize his gift as well. Therefore, we must care not only for ourselves but for the whole church.

CO-WORKERS

Concerning the matter of the co-workers, let me first relate one incident to you. A brother who was working in a certain place wanted to invite another brother to his locality to work. He came and asked me if he should make the invitation. I told him that he did not have to ask me but that he should consider whether or not the brother would be received if he were introduced to the assemblies in Peking, Shanghai, or Nanking. He was afraid that the brother would not be received. Then I told him that if that was the case, he could not receive this brother and invite him to work in his place either. If he recognized such a one as a co-worker, he would be bringing him into the work of his other co-workers as well. He should not receive a person on behalf of himself or the few who are meeting in his local assembly; he should receive him on behalf of the whole Body of Christ. If men like the apostle Paul were still living on earth, he would be receiving such a person as a co-worker on behalf of Paul, Peter, and others, and he would be adding a worker to them as well. If he did not receive in this way, he would be acting independently. All independent actions have no place in the Body of Christ and must be rejected. Every assembly has to be careful not to have an independent action but learn to follow God, so that the action of any one assembly becomes a joint responsibility of all the assemblies in other places.

NO CHANGE THROUGH MOVING TO ANOTHER LOCALITY

Suppose you have fellowship with a certain brother in Peking. If he comes to Shanghai, he should fellowship with us. It would be wrong if he came to Shanghai and did not fellowship with us. We have a brother by the name of Yu Shin-liang. When he was in Kuling, a few Western brothers often came to meet with him, and they had fellowship one with another. When Brother Yu came to Shanghai, two of these Western brothers also came to Shanghai. They were in Shanghai for a few months, but they never came to break bread with us. When I asked Brother Yu about these brothers, he told me that they had been in Shanghai for a few months. I asked why they would not come to Hardoon Road to break bread with us, and he answered that they did not come because they were too busy. However, they did not come because of other reasons, not because they were busy. This is to act independently; this is not the action of the Body. Since they had fellowship with Brother Yu in Kuling, why would they not fellowship with those who have fellowship with Brother Yu in Shanghai? If they had fellowship with Brother Yu in Kuling, they should be able to fellowship with all those who have fellowship with Brother Yu in Shanghai. They should not just fellowship with Brother Yu and refuse to fellowship with those who have fellowship with Brother Yu. When they fellowship with Brother Yu, they have chosen to fellowship not only with Brother Yu but also with all those who have fellowship with Brother Yu. They should not choose to fellowship only with some brothers in some meetings; they should choose to fellowship with those in all the other meetings who have fellowship with their meeting.

Suppose there is a meeting in Shanghai today. You may come to break bread because you think that this place is better than other places and that you can hear good messages here. As a result, you begin to communicate and fellowship with the brothers who are meeting here. A little while later, you may move to Peking. There you will find brothers who are in fellowship with us also. But their number may be only a handful, and the meetings may be weak. However, in Peking there may be another place with a famous speaker, who is eloquent but who does not fellowship with us. When you arrive in Peking, you may wonder in your heart whether you should meet with the very weak brothers or listen to the famous speaker. If you go to the place with the famous speaker, it is an independent action. When you fellowship with us, you have fellowshipped with all the brothers who have fellowshipped with us, and you cannot choose the place of meeting any longer. This is the principle of fellowship in the Body. You cannot act independently.

Many times, we think that if we could have our choice, we would change our place of meeting all the time. But there is no such thing as this. In the meetings, we have the greatest blessings, but we also bear the greatest responsibilities and have the greatest restrictions. If you go to Peking, you have to break bread at Brother Shu Tsong-jie's place. If you go to Tientsin, you have to break bread at Brother Lee Shun's place. If you go to Chefoo, you have to go to Brother Witness Lee's place. They are assemblies standing on the ground of the church. Do not think that the denominations bind people. Our fellowship binds people even more than the denominations bind people. What others have is an organization according to law. What we have is an organism in the Body. I am afraid that no denominations bind men as much as the principle of the organism of the Body, which we recognize. None of the members in our body can move freely for a day. Even a finger cannot have a day of freedom. The bondage we have is the bondage of the Body. As such, we have no personal freedom. Therefore, brothers, may we truly see the Body of Christ. If we see it, we will not act independently. After we have believed in the Lord, not only are we saved, but we also should act as brothers by standing in the position of a brother. We should not only be Christians, but among the brothers, we should behave as good brothers. Only then are we actually loving the brothers.

THE RESPONSIBILITY OF EVERY BROTHER

In practice, we have to ask: What responsibility should the brothers bear? Every brother should bear the responsibility not only of the local assembly but of the brothers and sisters who are in fellowship with them in the whole of China. Actually, he should care for those in the whole world who have fellowship with them. At present, we can only consider all those who have fellowship with us in China. But to be more scriptural, we should eliminate the thought of China and consider all the believers everywhere in the whole world who have fellowship with us. We share with them the same fellowship with God and His Son. One of our shortages is that we who meet in Shanghai only see the ones meeting in Shanghai, while those meeting in Peking only see the ones meeting in Peking. The greatest lack today is that believers do not have a world view and worldwide love. Many people only see their own sins; they only know that when they believe in the Lord, their sins are forgiven, and they are saved. They do not know what the fellowship among the brothers is. Many only see the brothers in their own localities and do not care for the brothers in all the places. This is not according to God's will.

God saves men in order to gain living stones for the building up of the spiritual house. If there were only individual, isolated stones, there would not be a spiritual house. Our breaking of the bread is a manifestation of the whole Body of Christ. Everyone who breaks bread should be responsible to the whole Body of Christ; he should see that he is responsible to all those who have fellowship with him. Therefore, every time we are about to receive a brother into our bread-breaking meeting, the responsible brothers should show him that the breaking of bread is for the discerning of the Body. It is not only a discerning of the Lord's body but a discerning of the *Body of Christ*. If we do not discern the Body, we are committing sin.

Therefore, all the brothers who are breaking bread should realize the scriptural requirement for breaking bread: (1) A person must be saved, and (2) he must not be one who commits the sins in 1 Corinthians 5. Moreover, he should know the responsibility he bears as a brother who partakes of the bread. He is responsible to the local brothers, and he is responsible to the assemblies in all places. If any brother is not clear about the responsibility he should bear, we should not reject him but allow him to consider, and we should show him the consequences of not bearing this responsibility. He should realize that the breaking of bread is not only for the remembrance of the Lord but also a matter of responsibility to the fellowship of the church. If a brother is clear about all these matters and is willing to take the responsibility, he can be received. Otherwise, we should allow him to consider carefully and think clearly. He should then make the decision by himself whether or not he wants to fellowship with us.

This is not a new invention. It was present two thousand years ago. If a brother wants to go to a certain place, he should first try to find the brothers who are in fellowship with us. Do not move to a place for four or five months without looking for the place to meet and without letting others know where you are. Before you leave your own locality, do not neglect to ask the elders to write a letter of recommendation for you. You have to realize that wherever you meet, you are responsible to that assembly. Your conduct there should be worthy of a brother. You should not act like one who is not a brother. If all of us take care of the mutual fellowship and act according to the Scriptures, our fellowship will become very precious. Our responsibility is to care for the whole Body of Christ, not only for the things related to the local assembly. We should not be like those in the denominations, who are pew members only, who do not care for others, and who do not know anyone else except the pastor. The Presbyterians only know the things related to Presbyterians, while the

Methodists only know the things related to Methodists. But we should be different. We should know all things related to all the brothers and sisters who are in fellowship with us; we should know the things related to all the brothers and sisters in the whole world. May God bring us to the position of the church at the beginning. May He show us this matter.

If a brother or a sister has the opportunity to go to another city, he or she should first investigate if there are brothers in that place who are in fellowship with us. If in that place there are two or three places that one can have fellowship with (such as the Brethren assemblies or other independent meetings), and if the choice is up to him, he should choose to fellowship with the brothers who have fellowship with us. This will bring benefit to their meetings and bring benefit to him as well. We admit that the way we take is a lonely way and that the number of those taking this way may not be large. But God will open doors for us so that everywhere we will find some people of the same mind who will meet with us. May God show us what the Bible requires of us.

RESPONSIBILITY AMONG THE ASSEMBLIES

The Bible tells us that a rule that God sets for one assembly is the same rule for another assembly. If the rule in two assemblies is different, there must be something wrong. Either the rule in one place is wrong or the rule in the other place is wrong. Of all the books of the Bible, 1 Corinthians is the clearest in dealing with the affairs concerning the church. First Corinthians 1:2 tells us that it is written not only to the believers in Corinth, but to *all those in every place* who call on the name of the Lord. In other words, all the churches should take the same way; it should not be different from one church to another. In 1 Corinthians the apostle taught about the sister's head covering. After he finished his teaching, he said, "But if anyone seems to be contentious, we do not have such a custom of being so, neither the *churches of God*" (11:16). The apostle did not allow the action of one local assembly to be different from another assembly. From this, we see that our meeting cannot act independently. Every assembly should care for the other assemblies. Before we do anything, we should consider how our actions will relate to the other assemblies. A sister cannot be free of her head covering in the meeting in Peking while covering her head in the meeting in Shanghai. In the churches of God everything has to be in one accord. In 1 Corinthians 14 it is said that women should not open their mouths in the meetings, "as in *all the churches* of the saints" (v. 33). This shows us that all the churches of the saints should keep the matter of sisters not preaching in the meetings.

However, the meetings in the various churches begin at different times: some begin earlier; others begin later. In addition, the condition of the various churches is also different. Some are clear about the truth of the church, while others are not so clear about the truth of the church. What then should we do? We should learn in a humble way to follow the other assemblies. The apostle said, "And you became imitators of us and of the Lord, having received the word in much affliction with joy of the Holy Spirit" (1 Thes. 1:6). Again he said, "For you, brothers, became imitators of the churches of God which are in Judea in Christ Jesus" (1 Thes. 2:14). This verse tells us that the church in Thessalonica were imitators of the churches in Judea. Why did the church in Thessalonica have to imitate the churches in Judea? It was because the gospel was first preached to the Jews. The Judean churches were the more "senior" churches. (I am taking the liberty to use this expression for now. Please note that the Bible never describes the churches in Judea in this way.) No assembly can act independently. Not only should individuals not act independently, but the whole assembly should not act independently.

INDEPENDENT ASSEMBLIES

If anyone wants to set up an assembly in a place and does not want to fellowship or communicate with other assemblies, he is not standing on the ground of the church. None of the churches in the Bible ignored the other churches. In other countries, among all the so-called churches, we have not yet found an assembly that is standing on the same ground of the church as we are. If there are such assemblies and we care only for the churches in China and refuse to communicate with these churches in foreign countries, we are wrong. With God, there is no difference between the churches in China and the churches in other countries. If we only care for the churches in China and cut off the churches in other countries, we are not walking according to God's will. The church of God can be found anywhere in the world. It is a different matter for a person to be unable to find an assembly that is meeting on the ground of the church. But if we try to limit our fellowship only to China, we have lost the ground of the Body.

WHAT IS A SECT?

I am afraid that some lawless believers will rise up among us, hoping to gain a name for themselves or to assume the authority of an elder. If they do not achieve their goal, they will go to another place like a village or an island and lead some people to salvation. They may eventually preach the gospel successfully in another place and lead many to salvation. They may proceed to help the saved ones to have meetings, break bread, and have elders and deacons. They may do all of these things according to the Bible, yet not fellowship with us. Instead, they will only care for their own meeting and hold tight to their "turf." They may think that they can ignore us and let each go his own way. Little do they realize, however, that they will become a sect by doing this; they are not an assembly that stands on the ground of the church. As mentioned in the Bible, they are actually a sect because their fellowship is limited to only the one or two hundred people among them. Even if the meetings, the breaking of bread, and the appointment of elders and deacons are all done according to the Scripture, it is still a sect if their fellowship is restricted to only one place. Therefore, in the future, if there is an assembly that has fellowship that is limited to only one locality, not based on the Body of Christ, and not inclusive of all the believers, it is a sect.

Why is Presbyterianism a sect? It is a sect because Presbyterians can fellowship only with the Presbyterians in Nanking, Soochow, England, or America. If a fellowship includes only the Presbyterians in Nanking, Soochow, England, or America and does not include the whole Body of Christ, that fellowship is a sect. Therefore, any fellowship that includes only a few local believers but does not include the whole Body of Christ at all times and in all places is a sect. If some lawless ones among us depart, set up another assembly, and restrict the believers' fellowship to their meetings alone, they will become a sect.

If the brothers in Chefoo adopt a closed attitude, work diligently, and ask the brothers to do everything according to the Bible, but do not fellowship with others, then sectarianism has to be dealt with all over again in Chefoo because they have become a sect. Every sect has its distinctive marks. If a man takes localism as a mark of distinction, he has become a sect. In considering whether an assembly is a sect or not, it is not enough to see whether its practice is scriptural. The main question does not involve whether or not the practice of an assembly is scriptural but whether the assembly itself is a sect. If it is a sect, we should depart from it. If an assembly is not of the Body of Christ nor for the Body of Christ, it should be forsaken because it is a sect. Therefore, if we want to serve God properly, we must learn how to not disobey God's commands and how to be restricted by the brothers and sisters. We cannot care for one place alone. All the churches should have the same practice toward certain matters. Yet the standard of our conduct is not according to the approval of the majority but according to the decision of the brothers in oneness. Oneness and one accord are the works of the Holy Spirit, while the consent of the majority emerges from man.

The principle of the Open Brethren is to care only for their own local assemblies, while ignoring the assemblies in other places. If a man is excommunicated from the assembly in Nanking, he can still break bread in the assembly in Shanghai. They even boast that they never argue with another assembly. If we follow their practice, Shanghai will care only for Shanghai, and Nanking will care only for Nanking. Of course, there will not be any arguments, and everyone will coexist in peace, doing their own work. Actually, the Open Brethren are not free from arguments. If a few have divergent views

concerning some doctrines within an assembly, they will split.
Perhaps by the following Sunday, they will have already separated into two meetings. One group may rent another place to
meet. In some localities, the brothers are divided into several
assemblies, and no assembly communicates with another
assembly. Yet they still tell others that they do not argue!
Those who prefer one kind of practice go to the assembly with
that kind of practice, and those who prefer another kind of
practice go to another assembly that has their preferred kind
of practice. This is no different than the way of the denominations. The only difference is that the denominations are larger
sects, while they are smaller sects. However, this is not the
way or the teaching of the Bible.

ONENESS IN ADMINISTRATION

If the assembly in Shanghai excommunicates a brother,
and the assembly in Nanking receives such a brother, we cannot cut off the assembly in Nanking altogether; we can only
negotiate with the assembly in Nanking. A person excommunicated from one local assembly is excommunicated from
all the assemblies, and a person received by one assembly
is received by all the assemblies. Not only do the assemblies which stand on the ground of the church practice this
way; even the denominations practice this way. All those
who are excommunicated by the Presbyterians in Shanghai
are excommunicated by the Presbyterians in Nanking. If the
denominations do this, should not we, who are standing on
the ground of the church and expecting the life of the Body of
Christ to be expressed, have mutual relationships which are
more intimate and more in oneness than those in the denominations?

However, we also have to pay attention to another side of
the truth. The administration of the assemblies is completely
local. Shanghai cannot overturn or interfere with the decisions of Tsinan, and Tsinan cannot overturn or interfere with
the decisions of Shanghai. However, in making decisions, both
Shanghai and Tsinan have to consider how their decisions
will affect the other assemblies. Therefore, we have to be careful and need to be bound for the sake of the other assemblies.

The administration of one assembly cannot be affected by other assemblies. But if this assembly is seeking after God's will in a definite way, it will not act presumptuously, using the excuse that the administration of churches is local; instead, it will consult the other assemblies, hoping to walk scripturally and according to the Lord's desire. All questions relate to whether or not our flesh has been dealt with and whether or not we are spiritual. In this way, we will be able to care for the other assemblies.

Suppose the assembly in Tsinan receives an unsaved person by mistake, and he is recommended to the assembly in Shanghai. On the day we receive the letter of recommendation, he becomes a person in Shanghai and has nothing to do with the administration in Tsinan anymore. From that point on, it is up to the assembly in Shanghai to deal with him or excommunicate him. The assembly in Shanghai does not have to ask the assembly in Tsinan concerning this matter. If the assembly in Shanghai excommunicates a brother by mistake, and the brother goes to Tsinan, the brothers in Tsinan may realize the mistake, but they cannot receive the brother excommunicated by Shanghai immediately. First, they have to write to Shanghai and check with the assembly in Shanghai. If the assembly in Shanghai does not agree with this matter, the assembly in Tsinan cannot receive that brother. But if the assembly in Shanghai consents, the assembly in Tsinan can receive that brother.

Therefore, it is a question of our flesh being put to the cross. Even between assemblies, this principle applies. If we are wrong, we have to submit to the brothers. But if we care only for our own proposals, the situation will become impossible, and we will become a sect. If a brother thinks that he can never be wrong, he has become a sect already. Therefore, we have to judge the flesh properly and put it to death so that we can live in the Holy Spirit and handle the affairs of the church in a proper way. If the flesh is not judged, and one wants to do one thing while another wants to do another, there will be no way to carry out the affairs of the church. All of us should deal with our self. This is true between persons, and it is also true between assemblies. This is the teaching of the Bible.

QUESTIONS

Question: Suppose a brother has a letter of recommendation from the church in Tsinan, and he comes to meet with the assembly in Shanghai. Later, if he is excommunicated by the assembly in Shanghai, should the brothers in Tsinan be consulted before he is excommunicated?

Answer: When the letter of recommendation is received, we should receive this person according to the letter of recommendation. Later, if we find out that this person is not yet saved, we can excommunicate him. Since the brothers in Tsinan are willing to recommend him, their decision must be right; we should believe in the words of the brothers in Tsinan absolutely and receive him initially. But if later we deal with this person and excommunicate him, we do not have to inform the brothers in Tsinan. This is like excommunicating a brother who has always been meeting in the assembly in Shanghai; there is no need to inform the brothers in Tsinan of such a decision. When that person comes to the assembly in Shanghai with a letter of recommendation, he is received by the brothers in Shanghai and is treated like all other brothers in Shanghai. When we accept a letter of recommendation from the brothers in Tsinan, we have accepted the brother, referred to in the letter, as a brother in Shanghai. Thereafter, the assembly in Shanghai has the authority to deal with him.

Question: Can we break bread in Kun-shan Garden? If we break bread there, are we acting contrary to the truth of the Bible?

Answer: At present, there are three tables in Shanghai. If we are not sure that the table in Hardoon Road is right, we should not come here tomorrow for the bread-breaking meeting. When we break bread at a table, we should acknowledge that it represents the whole Body of Christ. The table at Kun-shan Garden is of a certain group of the Exclusive Brethren. They have a closed attitude and communicate only with those who fellowship with them; they do not fellowship with everyone who has fellowship with God. Their fellowship includes only so many. Even if you are a very good brother, they will not receive you. You have to cut off your relationship with all other Christians before they will receive you. They are one of the seven or eight groups of Exclusive Brethren, and these seven or eight groups do not even receive one another.

If there are two bread-breaking meetings in one place, we have to distinguish which is the right one. If a meeting is raised up in one place, and another meeting is raised up in the same place, we cannot go to both places. We have to ask if the second meeting is also standing on the ground of the church. If both of them are standing on the ground of the church, they will surely fellowship with one another. This is like the relationship the meeting in Wen-teh Lane has with the meeting in Gordon Lane. Those who have been received by the meeting in Wen-teh Lane are also received by the meeting in Gordon Lane. The reverse is also true because we have only one fellowship. If we do not have the same fellowship, we cannot go to both places even when the form of the meetings in the two places is the same. We must investigate and determine which meeting represents the church and meets on the ground of the one Body. If a meeting is not meeting in this way, it is a sect.

When I was in America, it was right for me to break bread with Dr. and Mrs. Stearn. It would have been wrong if I had broken bread with those whom they would not recognize. The reason for this is that I had broken bread with them in Tsinan already. In a place where there is no assembly yet, we can act freely and set up the bread-breaking meeting. (Of course, we must also establish the oneness with the brothers whom we have fellowship with.) It would be wrong if I went to Hangchow and gathered a few people to set up a table, because there is a table in Hangchow already. Brother Luan would surely tell me that I should not set up another table. If that happened, I would need to confess my mistake. The Brethren say that they cannot receive anyone to their bread-breaking meeting who has not left the denominations. But this makes them another sect. As for us, we can fellowship with all those who are saved in the denominations. Suppose that there were no bread-breaking meeting in Ningpo. If two or three brothers went to Ningpo from Tsinan, they could start the bread-breaking meeting.

Question: In Peking, there is a bread-breaking meeting, but the brothers there are quite weak. Can I break bread there and also go to another place to listen to a famous speaker?

Answer: It is not absolutely wrong to go to another place to listen to some famous speakers. We do not forbid our people to go to other places to hear other speakers. But we have to make one thing clear: when you go to hear them, there is a limitation to your communication with them. If the goal of their works is not up to the standard of God's goal, their works are not God's work according to the biblical standard. I have said that God's work is not an evangelistic crusade, a society for the promotion of some cause, a Sunday school, or a revival campaign. From the beginning, God's work has been only one thing—the church. His work in every place is the building up of the local church in that place. Everything that comes short of this, that is, everything that endeavors for less than this goal, is not God's work. I am not saying that evangelistic crusades and Bible studies are bad. But if one only does these works and does not come up to the standard of the local church, he has not come up to the standard of God's goal. In reality, he is lowering the standard of God's goal. God's work in the book of Acts was nothing less than the local church; it never came short of this and never fell short of this goal.

Today, there are those in the church who preach the truth, lead others to salvation, or conduct Bible studies, preachings, or evangelistic meetings. Believers can do all of these things. But we have to lay hold of God's goal; we must come up to the standard of the church. I am afraid that although many works are good, they do not come up to the standard of God's work, which is the church. I believe there are many gifted ones who are not with us. I also believe that if we are more faithful, God will raise up gifted ones among us. If we live in God's light, there will not be the need for us to go to outsiders for messages.

Question: Some believers are critical of the truth we hold. They cling tenaciously to their own "Bible study," yet they want to break bread with us and even preach in our bread-breaking meeting. How should we deal with this kind of people?

Answer: If there is an exclusive Bible study meeting, it is not being conducted according to the principle of the church. Such a meeting does not come up to the standard of God's work. In other words, it is not God's work but man's imitation of God's work. God's work is always centered around the (local) church. It is good that man establishes Bible studies and evangelistic crusades; these are all blessed by God. But these things are not God's work. God's work has only one goal, which is the church. For example, the China Inland Mission is a mission; it is not a church. It is good for it to send men to the Chinese inland to preach the gospel; God blesses such a work. We probably do not have as much fruit as it has. But its work cannot be considered God's work. We can only say that God is working within its work. We should not ignore the working of God within its work. If we say that there is no working of God in their work, we will offend Him. However, the goal and the purpose of their meetings is not the local churches.

If people such as those you have just described want to come and break bread with us, we should be willing and happy to receive them. Yet we are not receiving their denominations. Although they are in the denominations, we should not reject them for this reason. However, our receiving does not mean that they do not need to leave the denominations. We should not refuse to receive a believer in the denominations; we should merely receive the believer himself. Afterward, we still need to advise him to leave the denominations.

If a man from the denominations is saved, we can receive him into the bread-breaking meeting. *But we cannot receive him to preach.* If anyone is not clear concerning the truth of the church, we can have fellowship with him only in life, but not in the work. Since he still has fellowship with the denominations, we do not know what he would speak if we allowed him to preach. Therefore, with many people, we can only have fellowship in life; we cannot be co-workers with them. This was the principle of the apostle Paul.

Romans 16:17 says, "Now I exhort you, brothers, to mark

those who make divisions and causes of stumbling contrary to the teaching which you have learned, and turn away from them." We should not listen to those who are here purposely to criticize us; we should turn away from them. In the future, when some brothers are raised up from the assembly to serve as elders, they can inform the other brothers as to whom they should turn away from and whom they should not turn away from. The other brothers should then obey the elders.

Question: Suppose I go to Sinkiang and suddenly discover a bread-breaking meeting that does not belong to any denomination. Should I start breaking bread with them, or should I first send a cable to Shanghai to get the approval before breaking bread with them?

Answer: There is good reason for doing the latter; it means that one respects the opinion of the brothers. At the same time, it shows how seriously you treat the matter. Sometimes, before you go to another place, you can first seek for the consensus of the brothers. The brothers may give you the liberty to join any bread-breaking meeting which is permissible to join. You can then break bread with them. As to the sending of a cable, it can be done if it is for the sake of informing the brothers or for understanding the brothers' mind. But it is unnecessary if it is done as a means of seeking approval. To understand the mind of the brothers is an act of the Body.

Question: Suppose I go to Sinkiang and realize that there is a bread-breaking meeting there which is related to the denominations, and I break bread with them. Later, when the assembly in Shanghai finds this out, how should it deal with me? Should I be punished or warned?

Answer: This is not just a hypothetical question you may face in Sinkiang; it is a problem we face right here in Shanghai. Let me ask you: For what purpose do you come to break bread here? If this table does not represent the Lord's table, and if you break bread just because others are breaking bread and remember the Lord just because others are remembering the Lord, what good will this bread do you? This does not mean that you can break bread with us only after you have stopped breaking bread with others. The question is how you view our table. If you do not think that this table is the Lord's table, why come to break bread with us? If you have found that this is the Lord's table, why look for another table? If anyone wants to do this, I must tell him that there is no such command in the Bible.

If anyone wants to break bread with us, yet at the same time, partake of the Holy Communion in the denominations, we cannot excommunicate him. But we should deal with this kind of person by exhorting him. If he would not listen to our exhortation, we have to act according to Titus 3:10, "A factious man, after a first and second admonition, refuse." Second Thessalonians 3:6 says, "Now we charge you, brothers, in the name of our Lord Jesus Christ, that you keep away from every brother walking disorderly and not according to the things which were handed down to you and which you received from us." We should leave these factious people outside our fellowship and not communicate with them, so that they will feel that they are isolated Christians. Of course, some are not this way intentionally; they behave this way because they lack knowledge. In such a case, it is altogether a different story.

Question: Sometimes I live in Shanghai and sometimes in Suchow. When the brothers in Suchow want me to do something for them, they consider me a brother in Suchow. Otherwise, they consider me a brother from Shanghai. Should I be considered as a brother from Shanghai or from Suchow?

Answer: Since you return to Suchow every year during the holidays and you feel that you should bear more responsibility for the meeting in Suchow, perhaps it is right for you to be considered as a brother in Suchow. Since you are in Suchow often, the brothers in Shanghai cannot consult with you about things concerning the assembly in Shanghai. I think you should consider yourself as a brother in Suchow. At present, the assembly in Suchow needs some responsible ones very much.

As to whether a brother should belong to this place or that place, we can say only that it depends on how long this brother stays in each place. Whatever place he stays in longer is the place he should belong to. Additionally, there are questions related to the boundary of the assembly. Concerning this last question, we will cover it in the next Monday night meeting.

Question: We know that when we receive a person, we have to ask him four questions: (1) Is he saved? (2) Does he have the obvious sins in 1 Corinthians 5? (3) Is he willing to be responsible to the meeting? (4) Is he willing to fellowship with the brothers? If a person is saved and does not have any obvious sins that forbid him from partaking of the bread, yet he does not want to be responsible to the meeting or fellowship with the brothers, and instead wants to control us, what should we do?

Answer: Please notice that the first and second points are our conditions for receiving a person to the Lord's table. The third and fourth points are for discerning the Body. If such a person does not discern the Body, he is eating judgment to himself. All who serve as elders in an assembly should be clear about this. Furthermore, there are two aspects to discerning the Body. First, we have to discern that this Body is the Body of the Lord Jesus and that when we break bread, we are eating and drinking for the remembrance of the Lord. Second, we have to discern this Body as the whole Body of Christ. When we gather together on the Lord's Day evening to break bread, we should realize not only that the ones who are breaking bread together are the Body of Christ, but that all those who are redeemed by the precious blood of the Lord are the Body of Christ. If a Japanese comes to our midst and breaks bread with us, we should acknowledge him as our dear brother just like all other brothers. If the British in Tibet start a war with China, and an English brother comes into our midst to break bread with us, we should regard him as our dear brother. We should not care for the distinction that exists between men but only for our relationship in the Body of Christ. If one who does not discern the Body comes to break bread with us, we can ask whether he is willing to discern the Body. Is he willing to be responsible to the church for all his actions? If he is not, we will not reject him from partaking of the bread, because he is saved. However, we have to let him know that if he does not discern the Body, he is eating judgment to himself and that it will be to his loss.

Question: Will one die if he eats judgment to himself?

Answer: Yes, he may. If a meeting is holy, and if it knows how to exercise God's authority, such things can happen. Why is the breaking of bread so important? When one recognizes the Body of Christ and acknowledges that he is a part of this Body yet does not discern it, he is making a false testimony and putting God to shame. Moreover, the testimony of the bread is made before angels, demons, and all the principalities and powers. Therefore, if one makes a false testimony, it is a great shame to God. God will bear with ignorant ones. But to those who sin willingly, who acknowledge yet make false testimonies, He will send forth His punishment.

Question: In a certain place, one brother has incurred a serious illness. He once committed the sin of reviling. Is his illness a punishment from God?

Answer: Yes, it is.

Question: If a brother is sick, must he ask the elders to anoint him with oil before he can be healed?

Answer: There are a few reasons why believers become sick. Some illnesses are caused by carelessness in the natural realm. Some are caused by attacks from Satan. Some are the result of being detached from the Body of Christ. If a believer is sick because of being detached from the Body of Christ and because he is not holding the Head and standing in the proper position in the Body of Christ, he should first understand how he has become detached before he asks the elders to anoint him with oil. The meaning of anointing with oil is to return to the proper position in the Body of Christ *through the Holy Spirit.* We all know that we are members in the Body of Christ. Just as a member in our body receives the circulation of blood and the life of our body, so the members of the Body of Christ receive the circulation of Christ's life and His blood. This is typified by the ointment which flows from Aaron's head to his whole body. As long as the members are standing in their proper positions, the ointment will flow to them; they will receive the protection of the ointment, and their sickness will be gone. All those who take the proper standing in the Body of Christ are under the anointing of the Head. The ointment is on Christ the Head, but it flows from the Head to us. When we have the ointment, we have health. Where there is ointment, there is life. Believers are sick because they fail and because they have become detached and separated from the Body of Christ. When this happens, the life and ointment of Christ will not be able to flow to them.

The book of James says that if anyone among us is sick, he can ask the elders of the church to anoint him with oil (5:14). It says to ask the elders to do the anointing. The gifted ones are useless because the elders represent the church, the Body of Christ. The anointing of the oil signifies the restoring of the sick believer back to the anointing of the Head. If you can bring a person back to the anointing of the Head, his sickness will be healed.

Question: If that is the case, can a person who represents the church go to the sick brother and anoint him? Will this heal the sick brother?

Answer: Yes, this can be done. But before the anointing is applied, there must first be the confession of sins and prayers. James says that we have to confess our sins to one another. The reason there is the need for confession is that the mutual relationship in the Body has been severed. There is the need of confession in order to remove the sin of detachment and return to the original position. If the detachment remains, it is useless even if there is the anointing. Therefore, one must first remove the detachment and thoroughly confess his criticisms of and offenses with the brothers. Before they can anoint others with oil, even the elders have to confess their sins to one another in order to remove any detachments and blockages and return to the proper relationship in the Body of Christ. Only then will the oil of Christ the Head flow onto the members.

Question: What kind of oil should we use for the anointing, and where should we apply the oil?

Answer: The best kind of oil is olive oil. But if one does not have olive oil, he can use any kind of oil. The oil should be applied to the head.

Question: How should one deal with a believer who has disturbed the meeting and been stopped by the elders but does not listen, but who has not committed the sins of 1 Corinthians 5?

Answer: We should inform the brothers to stay away from

him. The elders are those who are particularly charged to bear spiritual responsibility. If there are such people in a locality, the elders should be responsible to deal with them in their prayers. We have to know that it is a serious thing to deal with a brother in prayer. If a few responsible brothers would deal with such matters in one accord and in a sober way, many tragic, serious, and dangerous things can happen because God will use His appointed authority to judge. This is not a question of being good at prayer or not. When trouble arose in Corinth, Paul rebuked them for not being able to deal with the situation. This is why the elders have to be careful and deal with matters properly. If moral corruption in the flesh is not dealt with, such flesh will be destroyed. This will result in terrible consequences. Therefore, we have to learn to be obedient persons so that our flesh will be morally restrained and so that we will not cause any trouble.

Question: What does it mean to meet by standing on the ground of the church? How can we know that our meeting is standing on the ground of the church?

Answer: If you go to a new place and find an assembly in which baptism, the breaking of bread, the way of meeting, the place given to woman, and the appointment of elders and deacons are all done according to the Bible and which is the same as we are, you must not rashly join their table and their fellowship. I have to clarify one thing here: Concerning the matter of the breaking of bread and the fellowship, we are, at the same time, very open and very closed. We are open because all of God's children, as long as they are not disqualified from fellowship according to the Scripture, are received by us if they *come,* irrespective of what denominations they come from. We are closed because we cannot *go to others* for fellowship or the breaking of bread, as long as they are not standing on the ground of the church, no matter how scriptural in form their meeting may be.

If you find an assembly which is very scriptural in form and looks the same as we do, you must not presume that everything is the same and that we can join them. There is one *very* crucial question, which is whether or not the meeting is standing on the ground of the church. Before this question is properly answered, you cannot *go to them* and join them in the breaking of bread. The reason we do not go to the denominations to join them in the bread breaking is that they are not standing on the ground of the church. Their bread cannot represent the whole Body of Christ but merely their own denominations.

What does it mean to be "standing on the ground of the church"? Two things are very crucial.

(1) One must not be a sect. What is the difference between a sect and the church? The church includes all the believers, while a sect only includes a part of all the believers. A sect erects walls within the church and divides itself from the rest of those who belong to the church. A sect is not standing on the ground of the church, because it bears a name which is not shared by the whole church. It emphasizes special truths which the whole church does not necessarily emphasize, and it has a fellowship (with its members) which is not shared by the whole church. In order to stand on the ground of the church, an assembly must not have a name that is different from the general name of the church; it must not have any special truths or special membership.

(2) In order to stand on the ground of the church, one must live out the Body. If you come across a certain group which does not have a name, creed, or membership and which meets and practices other matters according to the Scripture and is the same as we are, you must still ask (even though it is not a sect) whether it is living out the Body life. Not every group that is not a sect is standing on the ground of the church. If a group is not a sect on the negative side, it does not necessarily follow that it knows the Body of Christ and the church of God on the positive side.

You must see whether an assembly can bear the responsibility of being the local church in that locality. If there are small meetings of similar nature in its locality, does this assembly strive to join itself to them to become the local church in that locality? Does it deal with them, teach them, and help them to realize the nature of a local church? Or does it ignore the issue and allow the situation to remain loose, disqualifying any of the meetings from becoming a representation of the local church? If there are independent free preachers in that locality who do not belong to any denominations, does this assembly take the initiative to guide and deal with such ones, so that there will not be isolated workers in that locality? Or does this assembly care only for itself and adopt an attitude of unconcern toward other workers? Is it trying its best to accommodate all of God's children, or is it digging deep ditches and building walls around its own small community? If it does these things, it is not standing on the ground of the church and not trying to bear the responsibility of being the local church in that locality.

In addition, even if an assembly has taken the responsibility of being the local church in that locality, one must still investigate whether it has adopted an attitude of "localism," in which it cares only for its own locality. Does such an assembly recognize that the church of God is universal and that it has to fellowship with other local assemblies who are standing on the ground of the church? If it does not want to fellowship with other local assemblies and bear the responsibility of walking in the same footsteps as the others, it is still not standing on the ground of the church. An assembly that stands on the ground of the church should be responsible for representing the members of the Body of Christ in that locality. It should try to fellowship with other members of the Body of Christ in other localities. (For further explanation, see the main text in this chapter.) If an assembly does all these things, it is standing on the ground of the church.

I believe you know that in the Bible there were originally only local churches. Today the (outward) church has degraded and fallen into serious divisions. Since there are so many denominations in one locality, no one meeting can claim to be the local church in that locality anymore. Therefore, we can only say that we are merely an assembly that stands on the ground of the local church; we are not "the local church." The reason we stand on the ground of the church is that so many of the existing denominational meetings are not standing on the ground of the church in that locality.

Question: If a table meeting is willing to receive all of

God's children, can we then say that such a meeting is standing on the ground of the church?

Answer: The first thing to settle is the meaning of standing on the ground of the church. We know that to stand on the ground of the church, one must not be a sect. Yet this is the negative aspect only. On the positive side, one must express the life of the Body of Christ. This means that one must not act independently, and *there must be the willingness to move together with all the brothers who are not in the sects.* Of course, we cannot take the same way as the brothers in the sects. Yet, even though the church is in ruins today, there are still those who desire to walk outside the sects and human organizations. We should take the same way together with those who are not in the sects. Only then can we say that we are standing on the ground of the church.

Strictly speaking, the expression "standing on the ground of the church" applies only to today, a time when the church has become degraded. When the church really becomes one, without sects or human organizations, everyone will be standing on the ground of the church and expressing the life of the Body of Christ. But at present, the (outward) church is in ruins, and men have divided themselves into sects and walk according to human ways. Therefore, there is the need for a group of people who will not only be non-sectarian *but* who will also stand on the ground of the church to express the proper life of the Body on behalf of the whole church.

In many places today, there are believers who see the error of the sects but *who do not see* the Body of Christ. They think that as long as there are no sects, nothing could be better. They do not realize that being rid of the sects is only the negative aspect. Although the church has lost its outward oneness, those who have left this disunity must still walk according to the principle of the oneness of the church in everything. Therefore, even when a table is willing to receive all of God's children, we must still ask if its work, testimony, and fellowship are joined to all those who have left the sects. It must not have the concept that because others have become sects, those who are left behind and do not want to be in a sect can no longer be one like those in the early days when there were no sects. All those who are not in the sects should express the proper Body life of the church. If anyone thinks that he is not in a sect but does not want to cooperate in work and fellowship with others who are not in a sect but would rather act independently, he is not standing on the ground of the church even though he receives all of God's children. He still does not know what the Body of Christ is. As such, that table is still not the Lord's table, because that bread cannot represent all the believers. Since its work does not include all of God's children, and in particular, those children who are not in the sects, we cannot participate in that bread. God has not excused us from expressing the Body life just because other members have divisions among themselves.

If a denomination is willing to openly receive all of God's children, can we go and fellowship with it? Surely we cannot. If there are brothers who are not in a sect in one place who do not fellowship with those who are not in a sect in another place, they are the same as the denominations and not standing on the ground of the church. In reality, they are another sect, and we cannot go and break bread with them. But this does not mean that we will not receive them when they come to us. It merely means that we cannot go to them.

Chapter Three

HOW TO MEET

There are several kinds of meetings, but we have to pay attention to two things with every meeting:

(1) *Come early.* Those who live upstairs in the meeting hall should not wait until the first hymn is sung downstairs before they come down for the meeting. Being late for a meeting is a very unkind thing because it means that others have to wait for you. First Corinthians 11:33 says, "So then, my brothers, when you come together to eat, wait for one another." Not many people practice this verse. Unfortunately, many do not come and wait for others; instead, they want the other brothers to wait for them. Sometimes we wait from 9:30 to 10:00, and some brothers still have not come. I will say a word especially to the brothers living in Wen-teh Lane. Those who live nearest to the meeting place are often the latest to arrive. Every one of us should try our best to be here early, so that others will not have to wait.

There are negative effects in coming late to the meetings. First, it causes a meeting to start late and end late. The sisters who bear the responsibility for their household are late in returning home, and this delays their cooking or care for their children. Second, during the bread-breaking meeting, another brother may have called a hymn already. Because you are late, you may come in and call the same hymn again, bringing in repetition. Third, sometimes the meeting begins before you arrive. When you come in late, you start the meeting all over again. This can happen four or five times in a meeting, with four or five different beginnings. Although we can learn to remember the Lord by following the leading of the Spirit and start the meeting for the remembrance of the Lord in different ways, sometimes with His suffering, sometimes with the forgiveness of sins, and sometimes with the Lord's glory, a person who is late to the meeting will not know how the meeting has begun, and his prayer and hymn selection will not be in line with the meeting. Therefore, it is better to come earlier and wait for a while in the meeting place. This is always better than coming late.

(2) *Stand up to speak.* For the bread-breaking meeting and other general meetings, it is better for the brothers to stand up to speak. According to Chinese custom, it is impolite for one to speak while sitting down. Moreover, one who speaks while sitting down cannot be loud, and it is difficult for others to hear him. In addition, his voice can easily conflict with the voices of other brothers. If you are sitting down with your head bowed and call a hymn, you cannot see if another brother has stood up to pray or call a hymn at the same time. At any rate, our ears are not as sharp as our eyes. If you stand up first, you can avoid the confusion of two people opening their mouths simultaneously. If two people open their mouths simultaneously, it is because both of them have not stood up before they opened their mouths. Therefore, we would like the brothers to remember that whenever they want to say something, whether it is praying or calling a hymn, they should first look with their eyes to see if anyone else has stood up before them. If no one has stood up, then it is all right for them to speak. Although these are small points, they are nevertheless things that the brothers should pay attention to.

THE BREAD-BREAKING MEETING

The first point we should emphasize is that we are at the bread-breaking meeting to remember the Lord. Therefore, the Lord should be the center. It is unsuitable to offer prayers and supplications at the bread-breaking meeting. Of course, we can thank and praise the Lord through our prayers, but we should not remember our own needs during the bread-breaking meeting. The meeting on the Lord's Day evening is purely for thanksgiving and praise.

According to the light of the Bible, there should be two sections to the bread-breaking meeting. Before the breaking of bread, we have the Lord Jesus before us; after the breaking of bread, we have the Father before us. Before the breaking of bread, the Lord leads us to remember Himself. Therefore, all thanksgiving and praise should have the Lord as the center; everything should be centered upon the Lord. Before the breaking of bread, we see the Lord Jesus as the only begotten Son; He is the only Son. After the breaking of bread, we see the Lord Jesus as the firstborn Son; we have a share in the Son of God and have become God's many sons. Before the breaking of bread, the Lord Jesus is one grain of wheat; after the breaking of bread, He is the grain that has fallen to the ground and died and brought forth many grains. By discerning the Body of Christ, we see the Lord as the firstborn Son, as depicted in Hebrews 2. He is leading many sons into glory, and in the assembly He is leading them to sing praises to the Father. This is what is described in Hymn No. 183 in our *Little Flock Hymnal*. But this should not be legal; it does not mean that every time we meet we should act this way. If we are willing to learn and follow the Lord's leading, we will be very clear that this kind of spiritual guidance always leads us step by step, onward to the Father. The Lord Jesus first led the disciples to eat the Feast of the Passover. Then they sang a hymn and went to the Mount of Olives. The Songs of Ascents recorded in the Psalms (see the headings of some psalms) were songs the Israelites sang at the Feast of the Passover after they ate the Passover dinner. They sang these songs while they were ascending the stairs. Therefore, after we partake of the Lord's body, we should ascend to the mountain to praise God. We should allow the Lord to lead us and draw us to the Father. All of our hymns are hymns of ascent. Our hymns should climb higher and higher after the breaking of bread. This is not just the teaching of the book of Hebrews. The Lord's word, the teaching of the Psalms, and our experience all testify to this. After our salvation, we always thank the Lord first, then praise Him, and then worship God.

The second point of emphasis is on learning to follow whatever has begun in the bread-breaking meeting. We are remembering the Lord, but there are many different beginnings for this kind of meeting. Some beginnings emphasize the Lord's sufferings, others emphasize the Lord's glory, and

still others emphasize what the Lord has passed through. We
have to pay attention to the way a meeting begins and follow
the same line. No hymn or prayer should come up with
another line of emphasis, but they should strengthen and
advance the existing line until the end. There should not be
three or four beginnings. Furthermore, we should never seek
for an opportunity to squeeze into the bread-breaking meeting the interesting passages that we have come across during
our morning Bible study time or the hymns that we like to
sing at other times. These are things that are related to us
personally and should not be things that we do as brothers.
We are not in the meeting to take care of our personal
relationship with the Lord but of the going on of the meeting
in oneness. This is a precious thing. Therefore, the bread-
breaking meeting tells us who the good brothers are. Do you
care only for your own things, or do you care for the move of
the meeting? Sometimes a meeting is about to end, and the
thanksgivings and praises are adequate, but a brother suddenly stands up to pray or call another hymn. This becomes
redundant.

In a meeting, you should cease from your personal activ-
ity and follow the move of the Body. If you are in a room
by yourself, you can sing or pray at will. But in a meeting,
you are not the only one who is present. Therefore, please
do not bring feelings that are peculiarly your own into the
meeting. Of course, all our thanksgivings and praises are personal; if they are not personal, they are not real and are a
speaking before others only. However, even though the meetings are very personal, we should care for the feeling of the
whole Body as well. This is why we have to follow a line of
emphasis.

The same is true with our preaching at the bread-breaking
meeting; we should have the Lord as the center. It is all right
for a brother to read a passage of Scripture which leads others
to the Lord or to remember the Lord. But there is no need to
read other unrelated passages of Scripture. There is no meeting that is as important as the bread-breaking meeting. When
we hear a message, we are merely listening to others speak
about the Lord, and the goal is for our own benefit. But the

bread-breaking meeting is the time when we meet the Lord and remember Him; it is a time reserved for the Lord Himself.

THE BIBLE STUDY MEETING

The brothers and sisters in Shanghai used to have a Bible study meeting. We studied the books of Romans, Ephesians, and 1 John. Unfortunately, this meeting has stopped for a few months. This kind of Bible study meeting is not for only one person to speak; it is for the brothers to study the Word together before God. Some brothers may open up a passage, while the other brothers may speak some, discuss some, ask questions, or supply explanations for that particular passage. In this way, verse by verse, a passage is covered, and the whole chapter is read and studied. Unfortunately, because no brother was particularly willing to take up the responsibility of the Bible study meeting, it stopped after a period of time. I feel that in the places where there is an assembly, it is a failure if we do not have a Bible study meeting. If there is to be a Bible study meeting, the brothers should be trained in this matter. The sisters should also do the same thing in the sisters' meeting according to the same principle.

There are no definite leaders in a Bible study meeting. Some brothers can read a passage, others can ask questions, while still others can answer or give interpretations. The principle of this meeting is that nothing is done for one's own benefit. No brother should involve his personal feelings in the meetings; they should all be left outside the door before entering the meeting. We have to take care of the expression of the Body life. This is true not only for the Bible study meeting but for all meetings. All the meetings are for the brothers. In the meetings, we are not expressing ourselves, and we should not wait passively for others to help us. In the meetings, we are here to *serve our brothers*. The Lord once said that the ones who are served are not great; rather, the ones who serve others are great. Every time we come to the meeting, we have to remember that we are here to be a servant to the brothers and sisters; we are here to serve the brothers and sisters and not just to listen to a message. Every time we come, we should consider ourselves as ones who serve and help the brothers. We should not have the proud thought that by doing this, we are greater and better than others. We do this because we ought to do this. Therefore, in this kind of meeting we should not wait for others to open their mouth. Perhaps we should open our mouth first to ask questions and show the other brothers something and then leave time for others to answer. In this way, everyone will be able to go on along the same line. If we realize that a question is adequately covered, we can go to another question. We have to remember that the purpose of these kinds of questions is not for taking care of ourselves or understanding something for ourselves. We should strive to make sure that the other brothers receive the benefit. Therefore, when we ask questions, we should not ask only questions that we want to ask and skip other questions that we already know the answers to. Although we may know many answers already, the new brothers may not know them. If we know the answers, we should ask on their behalf and express what they want to know in their hearts.

The message meeting is for helping strong Christians, while the Bible study meeting is *for helping weak believers.* In the message meetings, only those who can receive the message receive help; those who cannot receive the message do not receive help. The message meeting can be considered as being mostly for the knowledgeable or intelligent ones. (Of course, knowledge or wisdom depends on God, not on man.) Those who are foolish, illiterate, slow, or dull can receive only forty to fifty percent of what is released in the message meetings. The Bible study meeting is designed to help the weak believers. In the Bible study meeting you will realize how much your brother understands. You may think that some brothers ask unrelated or meaningless questions. You may think that they are dull. Actually, this is exactly what they need to know. Through their questions, you will learn what is affecting them or touching them. It may be a small thing to you, but to them it may be something great. It may be an insignificant thing to you, but to them it may be as great as a mountain. Therefore, do not think that the Bible study meeting is too shallow and of no help to you. You are there to help the meeting; you are there as a servant. Even the sisters, who do not open their mouths in the meeting, are there to help the meeting; they are there to serve the brothers and be the servants also. Perhaps your absence will become a loss for others. If everyone skips these meetings, the meetings will become small in number, and it will be a loss to the meeting. For you to come is to agree with this meeting and support the meeting.

I do not know if you realize that it is wrong for us not to help or serve the brothers and sisters. We care only for our own spiritual growth and do not want to help or serve the brothers; we do not care for the brothers' benefit or for the advancement of the meetings. The sisters should not think that they do not need to come anymore because they do not open their mouths and since they already understand the things being covered. Actually, their sitting in the meeting is a help to the meeting. Moreover, if some brothers feel that they know and understand a certain subject, they can ask questions on behalf of others and answer on behalf of others. They should not think that they understand the subject, considering it to be repetitious because they have heard it several times. I hope that the brothers and sisters learn to behave as brothers and sisters in the meetings and learn to behave as human beings among human beings. I hope that the brothers and sisters can have a common progress together. Therefore, I expect to resume the Bible study meeting among us within a short time.

In the meeting, do not raise controversial questions. During the past year, in all of our meetings, we have made progress and seen God's blessing in many aspects. But one day I saw a dreadful situation: two brothers were arguing about something to the extent that both were flushed with anger. They did not know how to behave as brothers among the brothers. The apostle said that we should not be involved with doubtful disputations. This is a very important principle. If you insist on arguing, you are doing wrong to your brother; you are not helping your brother but merely insisting on your own ideas. If you prevail in your own ideas yet have not rendered help to your brother, what good does that do? Therefore, in any kind of meeting, all of our flesh must be restrained, and all of our self must be put to death. It is easy to say this at other times, but our flesh encounters the greatest test in the meetings. At other times we may see the gentleness, love, and patience of a brother, but in the meetings we learn whether a brother is raw, sour, or sweet. Therefore, in the meetings we should try our best to drop doubtful things and not argue about them. Unfortunately, almost every brother thinks that his ideas should be accepted by others.

The only principle in the Bible study meeting is to drop the self. Being prideful or withdrawing in a meeting is an undesirable situation. Pride is looking at one's virtues; withdrawing is looking at one's own weakness and uselessness. If a person appreciates his own virtues, he will open his mouth often. If a person is conscious of his own weakness and uselessness, he will not open his mouth. Actually, it is equally bad to open one's mouth or close one's mouth. Where there is self, there is pride; where there is self, there is withdrawal. Both of these are the flesh and should be dropped. All questions should be for the Lord to receive the glory. As long as He has the glory, there should not be any problem.

THE GOSPEL-PREACHING MEETING

There is a big misconception among the brothers and sisters about the gospel-preaching meeting. I ask you to pardon me for bringing this up. Brothers often call and ask whether there is a gospel meeting in the morning or afternoon. What they mean is that if there is a gospel meeting, they will not come, because they are saved. This is wrong. Whether or not it is a gospel meeting is not the question. The question is whether or not you should go to the meeting to strengthen the hand of the brothers so that the brothers will not have to fight alone. Helping the brothers and coming to the meeting are not for our personal gain. Please remember that even though there is not an exciting and new gospel for one to listen to in the meeting, the gospel that is preached every time is a glorious gospel. A saved person should never feel tired of hearing the gospel. As long as you are sitting in the meeting, you are helping and strengthening the hand of the preaching one. If you have never had the experience of preaching, you will not realize the importance of this matter. If you have ever preached before, you will realize the comfort of seeing a brother sitting there. Therefore, in the gospel meetings, we do not expect to hear exciting, new truths. You may be familiar and well acquainted with many truths, but your presence helps and strengthens your brother. You are rendering help to the meeting and working together with God.

Once I met a brother who asked me whether or not there would be a gospel meeting in the afternoon. I said, "Yes." Immediately he said, "Ah!" That "ah" tells us a great deal. In the gospel meeting, the main thing is not to satisfy ourselves; it is not for us to receive the benefit. The main thing is for the brothers and sisters to receive the benefit and for the meeting to advance.

What is the expression on the faces of many brothers and sisters when they come to the gospel meeting? If there is some new truth concerning the gospel, their countenance is lifted up as they listen. But if there is nothing new, they may not say anything with their mouth, but they seem to be saying in their heart that they regret coming to the meeting, and their countenance is down. I am amazed that such a problem could exist in our gospel meeting. If it is God's gospel, we should feel that it is new even after hearing it the hundredth time. It is precious every time we mention God and His salvation! We should forever praise the gospel story.

Some brothers and sisters never show any expression on their faces. They are quiet; they neither laugh nor smile, and they are always cool and quiet. This kind of attitude does not render any help to the preaching brothers. On the contrary, it makes them feel very ill at ease. They do not know whether they have said something wrong to make the other brothers feel this way. If you have ever preached before, you will feel all these things. Many times, when brothers come to the meetings, they just sit and spread death. Even the expression on their faces makes the meeting cold. When you come to the meeting, it will not hurt if you say "amen" once in a while to show your sympathy. You may also nod your head or smile a little to indicate that you have received help from the word. If you do this, you are rendering the speaker some spiritual help. You will make him feel that the brothers are holding up his hands, keeping them from becoming tired, and that he is not standing alone. These are very important matters. The kind of attitude you have while sitting in the meeting directly affects the one who is speaking. Presently, the situation among us has much improved.

When some word from the preaching one touches you, it is most appropriate to say an "amen." I will not object to an even louder response. It is not just human beings who are saying "amen" within the house; the angels are saying "amen" also. This is similar to what is described in Acts 2 when Peter stood up to preach. I like that portion of the Scripture because it not only shows Peter standing to preach to the crowd; it also shows the eleven apostles standing with him. Even though only Peter opened his mouth, the eleven stood with him and were one with him. Therefore, in the gospel meeting, it is not a question of whether one lives a good personal life but whether his meeting life is proper. Please remember that we should not consider whether we have received anything or whether we are good or bad. If our meeting life is proper, our personal life will also be proper.

THE PRAYER MEETING

The number attending our prayer meeting is not very many. Of course, we have to do our best to forgive the brothers and sisters. Some live far away, and some are busy with other things. We can forgive them for not coming. But if we want to accomplish anything, and if we want to have the maximum power, the prayer meeting is where we can receive considerable help. The prayer meeting is the best test of our spiritual power. I hope that many brothers and sisters would attend this meeting and have the burden to pray.

The first thing we should take care of in the prayer meeting is to be punctual. The meeting life is a help to the spiritual life of a Christian; it is also an expression of the Body life of a Christian. If we do not pay attention to the meetings and do not care for the corporate life, we will surely fail.

In the prayer meeting, the things that are in need of prayer should be explained in simple and short words. One should not say too many words. This has been a failure of ours in the past. Every time we want to bring up a matter for prayer, we should ask ourselves whether or not we have prayed over the same matter at home. If we have not prayed over the matter at home, there is no need to bring it up in the meeting and deceive the brothers. If you have never prayed for something in your home, the need is not there, and there is no value in praying over it. This is a principle and even a law. Anything that has not been prayed over by you does not need to be prayed over at all. If you have prayed over a matter, yet feel inadequate when praying over it alone, it is worth mentioning in the prayer meeting; it is then a meaningful subject for prayer.

The prayers that God answers the most are the prayers that are offered at the prayer meetings. The prayers that God ignores the most are also the prayers that are offered at the prayer meetings. God often hears the prayers of individuals. As to the prayers in the prayer meeting, God hears them to a small degree as well as to a great degree. Men often use words in the prayer meeting which they do not use in their own room. They express sentiments which they do not express in their own room. One often does not have much to say or many things to cover. But when he comes to the prayer meeting, these words and things come. This is quite inappropriate. Anything that he does not have a burden to pray about in his room should not be brought up in the prayer meeting. All burdenless prayers are unnecessary prayers. All burdenless prayers are prayers that God never answers. If a prayer touches you, it touches God. If a prayer is accompanied by a burden within you, there is certainly a burden with God. If there is oneness and burden in our prayer during the prayer meeting, the power is surely greater than that of our individual prayers. Otherwise, there is no need for public prayer. All prayers that are unhindered, in oneness, and without barriers are effective prayers. God will surely listen to these prayers. This is why we call prayer a kind of work.

Prayers do not have to be long or numerous. We have to

build a net in our prayers, but one person alone does not have to build the net. If you feel that something has not been covered in the prayers, you should privately ask God to raise up others to pray and cast the net. When I was in England, one brother told me one story about a prayer meeting. One brother was burdened to pray for many things. He felt that his prayer was too long and that he ought to stop. Yet he felt that there were still many things that he had not prayed for. If he stopped, he was afraid that no one would follow after him to pray. If he went on praying, he was afraid that he would take up too much time. Being considerate of others, he felt that he should allow some other brothers to pray. As a result, he prayed, "I have prayed too long by myself. Please raise up another one to continue with my prayer." After he prayed, another person continued on with his prayer and uttered all the things that needed to be prayed about. Therefore, even if your mind is very strong, active, and sound, you should still ask God to raise up others to pray. God answers this prayer because He is a living God. In the prayer meeting, we should allow others to have a chance to pray. If we do this, there will be living prayers and prayers offered in one accord.

Sometimes God will use one of us to speak for the brothers and sisters. All those who are experienced in prayer know how difficult it is to find suitable utterance to express the needs. Although five or eight brothers pray for the same thing, the burden may not be released. Therefore, we have to ask the Lord to grant us the words to pray and express the thoughts in our burden. We should pray that God would raise up some to express His thoughts. Sometimes there can be as many as ten brothers praying for something, and all ten prayers can be good and up to standard, yet there is still the feeling that none of the prayers has hit the point, and the burden is not released. All of a sudden a brother may start praying and, as soon as he opens his mouth, the burden is released. Everyone feels right and says amen to it. This is a prayer in the Holy Spirit. In a prayer meeting, if no one expresses the inner need on behalf of everyone, that meeting is a failure. If we pray from 7:00 to 7:30 and successfully hit the point, we can go home; there is no need to go on praying, because we have reached the goal. The utterance of the Holy Spirit is the Holy Spirit's expression of God's desire through man's prayer. Only this kind of prayer can be considered a thorough prayer.

In the prayer meeting, there should be some brothers who act as the mouthpiece of the Holy Spirit. Sometimes five or six people may be praying for a certain matter, and they still cannot get through. But when someone opens his mouth, he touches the point. Then everyone feels that he has touched something real, and the blockage is gone. This is what we should pay attention to in the prayer meetings.

In 1926, I was seriously ill in Foochow. My whole body turned purple. Three brothers and a sister came to my room to pray for me. The first one prayed in tears, but I did not feel that he had hit the point. The second one also prayed earnestly for me, but I did not feel anything. The third one was supposedly famous for his prayers, but his prayer was still ineffective. The fourth one was the sister. When she opened her mouth, she said, "O God, no one can praise You in Hades. You have no pleasure in men praising You in Hades." Immediately I felt that something had broken through. I did not have to wait for the prayer to be finished before I felt that the sickness was gone. When the burden was lifted, I knew the sickness was gone. In the afternoon, I rose from my bed, and the next day I went to Ma-wei. From there I traveled to Amoy for my work. We have to ask God to use us to be a mouthpiece in the prayer meeting so that the burden and need of the brothers and sisters can be uttered through us with the language of the Holy Spirit.

Let me mention something concerning our last conference. Our conference was scheduled to begin on the Lord's Day, January 20. On Thursday evening, the seventeenth, we prayed during the prayer meeting for the needs of the conference. Many brothers did their best to pray for many things, and I did my best to say amen. Still there was a feeling that some kind of need or burden was not yet covered. Later one brother opened his mouth and said, "God, give us good weather which is not too cold, and do not let it snow or rain so that we can meet peaceably." Everyone there felt that his prayer received more amens than all the other prayers. The weather was not too good during those few days. The day when we had the prayer meeting, it was snowing. But by Friday, both the rain and snow stopped. It did not start raining again until the Thursday after the conference. During the whole period of the conference, there was no rain. Furthermore, in Wen-teh Lane, where we were meeting, another household was having a funeral. The Saturday before the conference began, the funeral ceremony was creating considerable noise and commotion. Yet the next day, it stopped. When the conference ended, the noise of chanting and music began again. If that had happened during the conference, we would not have been able to meet peaceably.

In the prayer meeting, there is the need for someone to be the mouthpiece of the Holy Spirit. If someone can be the mouthpiece, all problems will be gone. Our problem is that we do not know the needs. But God knows. Therefore, every brother and sister should strive to be the mouthpiece of the Holy Spirit. Whenever the prayers are thorough, the burden is released, and we know that there is no further need to pray.

THE BROTHERS' MEETING AND
THE SISTERS' MEETING

Since Shanghai is so large, the brothers and sisters are all scattered, and there is little fellowship between them. Therefore, there is a special need for the brothers' meeting and the sisters' meeting. Every Saturday afternoon at 4:30, we have the sisters' meeting. In the evening at 7:30, we have the brothers' meeting. During this kind of meeting, the emphasis is on mutual fellowship and on discussing ordinary affairs. We may talk about how the brothers ought to behave as brothers, and we may also cover something related to the meetings. In these meetings, we bring up problems of brothers and sisters who are out-of-town, problems of those who are unemployed, and other needs of the brothers and sisters, spiritual or material. This is very important. Through these meetings, we can avoid many mistakes and make many corrections. We cannot be individual believers before God; we have to learn to bear the responsibility of other brothers and sisters. A pew member in the denominations can remain a member for twenty years without knowing anyone. Some can be a pew member for five years without acknowledging anyone even once. Many people are only concerned about their personal salvation; they are concerned only about their Christian life and do not care for the other brothers and sisters. They do not care for the corporate life. But God has not made a heaven for each one of us and put us into our own heaven. Rather, He has put us in a corporate body so that we can help one another and fellowship with one another.

Many poor brothers dare not go into the houses of rich brothers. Many rich brothers do not like to go to the houses of poor brothers. In the world, there are distinctions between the rich and the poor, and in a family, there are distinctions between the master and the servants. But in the meeting, these distinctions should be removed. All differences in our position in the flesh should go through the cross. This is what the cross has done. We should not bring to the meeting what the cross has removed and put in the grave. The cross has not only removed the middle wall of partition between Jews and Greeks, barbarians and cultured ones, but it has also removed the separating wall between slaves and free men. In other words, all classes, ideologies, and systems that exist in society should be removed. In the family, there is a distinction between the master and the servants. But in the church there is no such distinction. If a brother is the servant of another brother, he is, of course, a servant at home and should be obedient to his master in everything. The brother who is the master should, of course, be a master at home. But in the brothers' meeting or the bread-breaking meeting, there is no distinction between master and servant. Both sides should avoid going to extremes. A servant should not think that just because he is a brother, he can tell others what to do at home. On the other hand, a master should not think that just because he is a brother, he should not rule over his servant in a proper way. In the family, there are differences of position. A Christian should still be a proper human being. For example, a father and a son may be Christians together. In the family, they are father and son. In the meeting, the son can call the father a brother. But in the family, the son cannot call his father a brother. Therefore, in the brothers' meeting, when brothers meet together, we should help the brothers understand that in the Lord there should be no question of being rich or poor, educated or uneducated, with status or without status. These distinctions should be removed. Therefore, the brothers and sisters should make an effort to come to the brothers' meeting and the sisters' meeting. These meetings are for fellowship, for helping the brothers and sisters solve their problems, and for living the corporate life. This is not a time for listening to sermons. Although there may be messages in these meetings, one does not meet for the sake of listening to messages. Otherwise, the meeting would be disbanded if the speaker went to sleep. The danger with many revival campaigns is that as soon as the revivalist is gone, the people are gone. God's way is to save individuals and put them into the church so that they can be blended together and help each other.

Since this is a matter of practice, I have to say a few words that may not be so nice to some. First, there should be more communication between the brothers not only for mutual care but for mutual oversight. Some matters should, of course, be handled individually. But with other matters, there is a need for us to know our brothers' problems. Suppose a brother has lost his job. We should find out how he lost his job and the reason for it. If it was a proper and honest layoff, we should bring this matter up in the brothers' meeting and help the brother according to the teaching of James 2. The main thing is to do something and not just to believe. It is useless to believe as the one in James 2. If a brother has lost his job through dishonesty, we should help this brother, exhort him, and deal with him. If he is truly unemployed, we should try to support him. Things like this cannot be brought up in the prayer meeting, the bread-breaking meeting, or the gospel meeting. We can bring them up only in the brothers' meeting. If there is anything that is related to personal reputation, which does not need to be announced in the brothers' meeting, then it should not be announced in the meeting.

It is wrong for us to be ignorant of the weaknesses and problems of the brothers, to not know whether a family has encountered difficulties, to be ignorant of the spiritual problems, needs, and sicknesses of others, and to fail to care for these ones. The denominations have hired pastors to do this work. But we do not have this class of people; every one of us has to take up this work. Poor brothers should not purposely try to avoid rich brothers, and rich brothers should not ignore the need of poor brothers. None of us can give up being a brother just because we do not want to communicate with certain ones. The brothers should express the assembly life through the communal life, and they should express the proper life of brothers. All those who do not see this are bound to fail, because this is what God wants us to do today.

QUESTIONS

Question: What does the meeting in 1 Corinthians 14 refer to?

Answer: The meeting in 1 Corinthians 14 is a meeting for the exercise of spiritual gifts. Our Saturday meeting is somewhat similar in nature to this kind of meeting. Today we do not have the kind of spiritual gifts that were present in the early days. We are merely meeting according to that principle.

Question: Hebrews 10 mentions not forsaking our assembling together. What kind of meeting does this refer to?

Answer: It refers to all kinds of meetings, including the brothers' and sisters' meetings.

Question: When should we break the bread during the bread-breaking meeting?

Answer: The breaking of bread is for the remembrance of the Lord. Therefore, we should break the bread as soon as possible. We do not have to always wait for Eutychus to fall down before breaking the bread. During the bread-breaking meeting, we should look for the high point of the meeting. Since everyone has different circumstances, family backgrounds, and environments and because everyone has different problems, failures, and weaknesses, bringing these things to the meetings is unavoidable. Therefore, concerning the bread-breaking meeting, some should begin the meeting by calling a hymn or by praying; this helps bring everyone out of their distractions and helps them forget about all the things that have happened during the past six days. The high point of the meeting is when someone prays and brings everyone up to a certain point, and everyone is released and says amen. That is the time to break the bread. We cannot break the bread immediately after we come together, because we are weak. It is common for us to bring our circumstances, family, and other things to the meeting, which frustrates our oneness. Therefore, we cannot break the bread immediately. There is a need for someone to bring us to a certain point, a climax, before we can break the bread. If we delay breaking the bread then, we will recede from that high point. Therefore, we have to take care to break the bread as soon as the high point is reached.

Question: Should offerings be made during the Lord's Day bread-breaking meeting?

Answer: It does not matter very much one way or the other. Of course, it is the Lord's commandment that we offer our money on the first day of the week. On the first day of the week, all the brothers and sisters, including all the workers, should offer. If they do not, they have disobeyed the Lord's command. Both the breaking of bread and the offering of money should be done on this day, but they do not have to be done in the same meeting.

Question: Should the bread-breaking meeting be in the morning, afternoon, or evening?

Answer: The teaching of the New Testament is that it should be in the evening. The Lord's supper should be eaten in the evening. Generally speaking, we eat breakfast quickly because we are in a hurry to go to work. Lunch is a meal eaten in the middle of our labor. This is why many people eat lunch at their place of work and do not go home for lunch. Only dinner is the family meal, in which the whole family gathers together to eat in peace and joy. For the sake of the brothers who are responsible for preaching, it is also better for the bread-breaking meeting to be in the evening. If the bread-breaking meeting is in the morning, those brothers will try to eat in a hurry because they have many burdens they have to release through their message. If we break bread in the evening, they can sit comfortably at the Lord's table.

Personally, I feel that it is better to break the bread in the evening, particularly in China. Of course, this will present some inconvenience to the sisters. In all the denominations in China, the services are conducted in the morning or afternoon. The members have developed the habit of attending services in the morning or afternoon. If our bread-breaking meeting is in the morning or afternoon, it is difficult to deal with these ones; if we allow them to partake of the bread, we are not sure whether they are saved. But if we do not allow them to partake of the bread, we may offend them. If we break the bread in the evening, there will not be such an inconvenience. If they come, they will find that there is no message. Moreover, the distance it takes to come to the meeting is great, and it will be late by the time they return home. As a result, they will not come. This is why we say that the bread-breaking meeting in Shanghai is best conducted in the evening.

Question: When we break the bread, do we have to lift the cup to bless it as it says in 1 Corinthians 11?

Answer: The matter of lifting the cup is a Catholic tradition. Catholic priests claim to bless the cup on behalf of the Lord Jesus. Therefore, when they lift up the cup, they speak in place of the Lord: "This is My body, which is broken for you. This is My blood, which is shed for you." Some Protestant denominations such as the Anglican Church, Presbyterian Church, and Methodist Church also do the same thing. Our present practice tells us that we cannot bless on behalf of the Lord. We believe that the Lord is among us and that He is still blessing the cup. When we bless, we are merely speaking on behalf of the brothers and sisters to the Lord: "Thank You, Lord." We believe that this is scriptural (1 Cor. 10:16). If any brother stands on behalf of the Lord Jesus, this usurps the Lord's position too much. The brothers among us merely serve as the spokesmen of the other brothers, thanking and praising the Lord this way. Since this is the case, there is no need to lift up the bread and the cup. Any brother who is in fellowship with us and who is not hindered by any evil, can stand up and give thanks for the bread on behalf of the other brothers.

Question: Should we stand up, sit down, or kneel down when we pray? If we do not kneel down when we pray, does this mean that we are being disrespectful?

Answer: There are many different ways to pray. The reason we do not kneel down is that the place is too small and would present a problem if we all knelt down. Moreover, the Bible never tells us whether we should pray by sitting down, kneeling down, or standing up. The Bible does not consider it disrespectful to pray without kneeling down, and it does not consider kneeling as the sole condition for praying. The worshippers of Buddha in China are the only ones who have to kneel down when they worship. The Bible records the Ephesian believers sending Paul off by kneeling to pray at the seashore. However, in Matthew, the Lord teaches men to pray by shutting their doors (6:6); He did not say to kneel down. The Bible often mentions praying by covering up one's face, and a few times it mentions praying by sitting before the Lord. The Bible also mentions praying by lifting up one's hands. For example, Moses lifted up his hands on the mountain. In fact, the Bible often mentions praying with uplifted hands. Lifting up one's hands is a sign of beseeching God. Therefore, when one lifts up his hands, it means he is invoking God's attention. This is why Paul told Timothy to "pray in every place, lifting up holy hands" (1 Tim. 2:8). One can pray in every place. But it is not easy to pray in every place by kneeling down. It is not difficult to lift up one's hands in prayer. But it is impossible to kneel down everywhere because, in some places, one cannot kneel down. Personally, I think this matter should be left to each person's own conscience. If a brother feels in his conscience that he should pray by kneeling down, he should do so. But there is no need to consider kneeling as a law.

Question: Can we forbid "outside" brothers from preaching at will in our meetings?

Answer: We should pray and ask God to stop the disenchanted ones in the denominations from coming into our midst. We are not for numbers. We should deal seriously with this matter so that the disenchanted ones in the denominations will not come and express anything in our meetings.

Question: Who should prepare the bread for the bread-breaking meeting?

Answer: According to the Bible, the preparation of the bread should be done by the deacons. There is no difference between a deacon and a deaconess; either a deacon or a deaconess can prepare the bread.

Question: Should the bread and the cup used in the bread-breaking meeting be covered with a piece of cloth, and should the table also be covered with a tablecloth?

Answer: The practice of covering the cup and the bread with a piece of cloth is a Catholic tradition. The Catholics think that if they do not cover them, they will not be holy. But according to 1 Corinthians 11, it is wrong to cover them. The breaking of bread is a display of the Lord's death; it is for *exhibiting* the Lord's death, and it is a testimony. Why then should it be covered? As to the tablecloth, there is complete liberty as to what one wants to do. If the table is not too clean, it is all right to cover it with a tablecloth.

Question: If it is a biblical teaching for the sisters to cover their head, why do we not practice kissing each other with a holy kiss since the latter is also a biblical command?

Answer: The Bible says that we should kiss each other with a holy kiss (1 Cor. 16:20); it does not charge believers to merely kiss each other. The command of the Bible is that if anyone greets another with a kiss, the kiss should be holy. God's command is that when we kiss, we have to be holy. He has not charged us merely to kiss. Neither have the apostles charged everyone to kiss. Kissing can very easily become unholy; therefore, there is the charge to kiss with a holy kiss. If anyone were to ask me whether we should kiss, I would say we should. But the Bible also tells us that if we kiss, we have to be holy. The emphasis of this command is to be holy and not just to kiss. If one kisses, he should be holy. Provided we are holy, I believe it is right for us to practice this biblical command—to kiss each other.

As to the sisters covering their heads, there are many

benefits to the practice. In the meetings, the sisters should have the sign of submission to authority for the sake of the angels (11:10). In the original language, the word *authority* in 1 Corinthians 11:10 refers to a positional authority. It is a positional authority because Satan was also an angel. The first sin of Satan was his "self"; that was the cause of his fall. When his self was expressed, he overturned God's authority and rebelled against God. The most amazing thing in the universe is authority. We must see that God works through authority. He upholds the universe with His word. The name of Christ is authority. God has placed Satan under His own authority, yet Satan overturned this authority. The great dragon mentioned in Revelation is the old serpent; he dragged along with him one third of the stars of heaven (12:4). This means that Satan led one third of the angels in heaven to rebel against God and overturn God's sovereign rule. This is known throughout the universe. This is the story of the first introduction of sin into the universe.

How did sin come into the world the second time? It came in through Eve. God created Eve and ordained that Adam should be the head of Eve. Paul said in 1 Timothy that it was not Adam who was deceived, but Eve (2:14). Therefore, the sin in the garden of Eden was the same sin that Satan committed. This sin came in when the woman rebelled against Adam, the head, and did something before she was approved by Adam. Therefore, sin comes from insubordination to authority; sin is lawlessness.

Because both Satan and Eve fell this way, God ordained that there should be a sign on the head of the woman as a symbol of submission for the sake of the angels. This is a testimony before the angels, showing the angels that we will not do what Eve did at the beginning. Of course, many sisters cannot take this. This is the greatest test to the sisters. If the flesh is willing to be judged, everything is all right. Today, we will mention the head covering only in relationship to authority. There are other aspects of head covering which we will not cover today. In the garden of Eden, the woman refused to remain in her position. Today in the church, our sisters should be faithful to remain in their own position.

Question: Should we tell the sisters who have cut their hair to cover their head?

Answer: These minor questions are a great test to our conscience. First, we should exhort the sisters who want to cut their hair to keep their hair. If they intend to cut it, we do not have to advise them to cover their head anymore because they have clearly given up the glory which God gives to them. There are two coverings for the sisters: One is a natural covering, and the other is a symbolic covering. If a woman gives up her natural covering, the symbolic covering will be completely useless to her. The symbol on the head must be put on willingly.

Question: When a brother prays or preaches on the street, should he take off his hat?

Answer: According to my personal experience, every time I pray, I take off my hat. I feel that if I do not take off my hat, I am shaming my head. But this does not mean that God will not hear us if our brothers pray with their heads covered and our sisters pray with their heads uncovered. Our prayer and prophesying are particularly related to the angels and the spiritual realm. Therefore, personally, I feel that the brothers should not cover their head. Even when we are preaching to someone on the street, it is related to the spiritual realm; as such, it is not that proper to keep our hat on.

Question: What is the difference between preaching and prophesying?

Answer: All those who can preach edifying messages may not be prophets. A prophet is able not only to edify others, but also to foretell. A prophet is able not only to declare God's will, but also to foretell.

Question: What should we do with the bread and grape juice after the bread-breaking meeting?

Answer: They can be consumed by one or two brothers, or they can be burned in the fire.

Question: In breaking the bread, should we break some off from the whole piece, or can we eat from the crumbs on the plate?

Answer: Both are all right; there is no difference between the two. They are all from the same piece of bread.

CHAPTER FOUR

THE BOUNDARY OF THE LOCAL ASSEMBLY

Tonight we will discuss the mutual relationship between the meeting in Gordon Lane and that in Wen-teh Lane. In other words, we will speak on the boundary of the local church or the extent of the border of the local church. Before we speak on this matter, there are a few things which we need to explain to the brothers from out of town. Our Bible study, at this moment, is designed especially for the local brothers. Therefore, many of the things that are covered are local in nature. However, we welcome the out-of-town brothers to come and listen.

I have mentioned three to five times already that the authority of the elders is for the local assembly. In other words, the elders are for the local assembly. Position is a matter related to the local church, and office is also a matter related to the local church. One can be an elder in Shanghai, but he cannot automatically be an elder when he goes to Nanking or Peking. A person who serves as an elder in the assembly in Shanghai cannot go to the assembly in Peking and assume the same eldership. God's gifts are for the whole church, while His offices are for the local churches. Hence, there is no such thing as a super elder who can control an out-of-town church. An elder can oversee only the church in his own locality.

THE BOUNDARY OF THE ASSEMBLY

The Bible study tonight is on the boundary of the assembly, and it is limited to the local assembly only. We hope that God will show us this truth. Because we are afraid of careless misunderstandings or forgetfulness, we will repeat once again what we have mentioned: gifts are for the whole church, while offices are for the local churches.

What is the extent of a local church? How big of an area

constitutes the sphere of a local church? We would draw the brothers' and sisters' attention to the fact that in the Bible, the church is never divided into regions. The Bible never groups a few churches together under a regional organization. Although there were seven churches in Asia, we do not see the Bible appointing Ephesus or Philadelphia to rule over the other six churches. We only see *seven* churches, with *seven* lampstands. These seven lampstands represent the seven churches (Rev. 1:12, 20). In the Old Testament, one lampstand was divided into seven branches. In the New Testament, there are seven lampstands, not one lampstand with seven branches. This means that the seven different churches are shining *by themselves* and each one is responsible to Christ *by itself.* Every church is governed by Christ alone and is not under the control of any other church. In administration, every lampstand is independent and not under the control of any other lampstand. Every one of them is responsible to the Son of Man alone, who walks in the midst of the seven lampstands. They are responsible only to their High Priest. No church is responsible to another church. Although they are seven churches, they have not joined themselves to become one united church, and they are not responsible to some higher synod or convention. Each one of them is a so-called congregation, an assembly whose boundary is the locality. The Bible takes the city or the smallest administrative unit as the boundary of a local church. A local church is the basic unit of the church in the Bible. No local church is joined to another church or regards another bigger church as the central church. In other words, in God's eyes, Rome has never been appointed to be the central church. God has never acknowledged one place as the center of all churches, with that place ruling over and controlling all the other assemblies. According to God's organization, there is no center on earth. Jerusalem was not the central church at that time.

This does not mean that there are no regions in the Bible. Some places have similar conditions and needs, and they are treated according to the same principle. In Acts 19 Paul "passed through the upper districts" (v. 1). In Romans 15 Paul said that he traveled "from Jerusalem and round about to

Illyricum" (v. 19). These places belong to one region. Galatia was not an individual city but a province. This is why the Bible mentions "the churches of Galatia" (Gal. 1:2). Revelation mentions "the seven churches which are in Asia" (1:4). Ephesus, Smyrna, Pergamos, Thyatira, Sardis, Philadelphia, and Laodicea were all in the region of Asia. Asia was a region, and Galatia was a province. We have to be clear that even though the needs and testimony of these local assemblies are peculiarly similar, no church possessed a higher organization or authority over the other local churches. The Bible never shows us that any local assembly possesses a higher authority than another assembly. Some have thought that Jerusalem was a mother church. Actually, there is no such thing. Every local assembly is local in its administration and responsible to Christ alone; it is not responsible to any other institution or assembly. Putting it another way, a local church is the only organization in that locality. To put it still another way, a local church is the highest organization and institution on earth; nothing is lower than it on earth, and nothing is higher. There is no court above the local church to which one can appeal. The highest organization is the local assembly. The smallest unit is also the local assembly. The Bible does not tell us of a center like Rome, which controlled everything of the churches, because Christ wants to retain His headship in heaven. Every local church should maintain the testimony of the Body and express the Body of Christ in a miniature way. However, every local church should be directly responsible to Christ and not to other churches. This means every local church should only be regulated by Christ and not be controlled by any other institutions or churches.

God dislikes the fact that man can be misled to think that there must be centers on earth. Therefore, He put Jerusalem aside and made Antioch the place from which the apostles set off for their work (Acts 13). It was not Jerusalem. This avoided the misunderstanding that the church in Jerusalem was the mother church, the headquarters church, and that all the other churches were subordinate churches and branch churches. Two hundred years ago the Brethren almost took London as their headquarters. This is a mistake. Therefore, brothers, please do not consider the assembly in Shanghai as the mother church or the headquarters. Our assemblies in the different localities are directly bound by Christ and are not controlled by any other assemblies.

The truth that I am speaking of tonight balances the truth that was mentioned last Saturday evening. Last Saturday night we mentioned the Body life and the relationship between an assembly and other assemblies. God will never tell one assembly to do something and another assembly not to do the same thing. The way God leads one assembly is the way He leads other assemblies. We saw that the Gentile churches should imitate the churches in Judea. We also saw that, according to God's ordination, no church of God should act independently; rather it should pay attention to the move of the Body and seek for mutual harmony. Any person that one assembly excommunicates should be excommunicated by other assemblies. Today we are speaking on the responsibility of a local church; its responsibility is to God alone and not to any other local assembly. What we covered on Saturday shows us the strictness of the bondage and restrictions between one assembly and other assemblies; no assembly can act independently or make its own proposals. If an assembly acts independently or makes free proposals, these acts and moves are not of God. At the same time, we must see that every church is directly responsible to the Head for what it does. We can easily become biased. This is why we must maintain the balance in the truth.

Sometimes, we may act like the Roman Catholic Church. When Rome makes a decision to do one thing, all the Roman Catholics in every place have to obey. This is not being balanced in the truth. On the one hand, we should be bound by other assemblies so that we have the same footsteps and are the same as far as the truth goes. On the other hand, every assembly should be directly responsible to the Head for what it does. Every local church is responsible to God. Every church mentioned in Revelation 2 and 3, like the church in Ephesus, the church in Smyrna, and the church in Pergamos, etc., had its own golden lampstand. Each stood on its own stand, not on another stand. Every one of them kept their own position and was responsible to God. The Lord both rebuked and praised Ephesus. He did not lay the blame of Ephesus on Pergamos, nor did He credit the virtue of Ephesus to Smyrna. No church can take the responsibility of another church, and no church can stand on the merit of another church. All the churches are responsible to the Lord directly and are bound by the Lord. At the same time, the Bible says, "He who has an ear, let him hear what the Spirit says *to the churches*" (Rev. 2:7, 11, 17, 29; 3:6, 13, 22). This is the balance in the truth. On the one hand, the Bible says that the words are spoken to the messenger of the church in Ephesus. But at the end of the speaking, it says that the words are for all the churches. At the beginning it says that the words are for the messengers of the church in Ephesus, the church in Smyrna, the church in Pergamos, etc., but at the end it says that every church should hear what God says to the other churches. The *Holy Spirit* is speaking to all the churches. This is why he who has an ear should hear. This proves that what is kept by one church should be kept by all the churches. The responsibility each church bears in a locality is before God alone, yet all the churches should have the same common move. Consequently, the epistle was written to Ephesus, but the words were for all the churches. This is the balance in the truth.

In the Bible God has ordained that the smallest unit of the church on the earth is the local assembly. The highest institution is also the local assembly. The local church is the ultimate and minimal organization. Every local church is a miniature to express the universal church. Nothing is bigger than the local church, and nothing is smaller than the local church. We should firmly grasp this truth. We should pursue and take care that what we do in the assembly in Shanghai, our move and footsteps, is the same as the move and footsteps of all the assemblies in China. Not only should we pursue having the same move and footsteps as all the assemblies in China, but we should also pursue having the same move and footsteps as all the assemblies in the world. At the same time, what we do in the assembly in Shanghai and whether we are right or wrong is something for which we are directly responsible to God. We are not directed by any higher institution above Shanghai. In the assembly in Shanghai, no authority is higher than the authority of the elders. This is the boundary that God has set. Within each city, there can be a few elders. But these elders can oversee only the assembly in that city; they cannot oversee the assembly in another city. God's boundary is based on the fact that elders are appointed in every city. This is why the authority of an elder cannot extend beyond the boundary of the city. The local churches as depicted in the Bible are local in their administration. I hope that the brothers and sisters maintain these two aspects in a balanced way. On the one hand, we maintain a sameness with the other assemblies. On the other hand, each local assembly bears a direct responsibility to God.

THE BOUNDARY OF A LOCAL CHURCH

I would like you to pay attention to the fact that in the New Testament, the boundary of the local church is the city in which that church is located. Hence, the maximum reach of a local church is the city; *no* boundary can be larger than the city. In the Bible we cannot find a church that rules over one province or county. The Bible shows us that the city is the boundary of the church. In the beginning the city was the community where men aggregated. We should remember that in the complicated situation of our modern life, there are many towns and villages. At the beginning, when families bound themselves together and set up protection, there were cities (Gen. 4:17). Due to various reasons, men began to dwell in cities. In the first half of the book of Genesis, we see no unit smaller than the city. By the time of Joshua, men still lived in cities. Of course, by then, there were neighboring villages. When the Lord Jesus sent the disciples to preach the gospel, He charged them to go into the cities and villages (Matt. 10:11). This is because a city or a village is the smallest unit of human habitation in the Bible.

The scriptural boundary of a local church is the boundary of a city. Ephesus, Corinth, and Thessalonica were all cities. The boundary of a local church cannot be larger than a city. Asia was a big area, and it had *seven* churches. Galatia was a region, and it had *churches*. Corinth was one city, and therefore, the Bible mentions the whole church coming together *in one place* (1 Cor. 14:23). The church in Corinth was one church. All the other local churches mentioned in the Bible had the city as their boundary. This is God's wise way to preserve the believers from much confusion. If God were to make the nation the boundary of the church, such a boundary would be changing all the time because nations often fall. If a nation fell, the boundary of the church would be changed. If God made a province the boundary of the church, the provincial boundaries would change often also. If the boundary of a province changed, the boundary of a church would have to change as well. Would this not cause some problems? This is why God has not made a province the unit of the church, nor has He made a nation or other political units the boundary of the church. Dynasties, nations, and provinces all change easily. God has made the city or village the boundary of the church because the names and boundaries of these places do not change easily. National boundaries constantly change, and the names of provinces constantly change. But the boundaries and names of cities and villages are least likely to change with political shifts. They are least affected by political changes; we can almost say that they are never affected by political changes. In many instances, a village was called by a certain name a few hundred years ago, and it is still called by the same name today. Many cities change hands from one nation to another, yet the cities themselves remain the same. The city (and to a greater extent the village) is the most stable unit politically. This is why God ordained the city to be the boundary of a local church.

There are advantages to God making the city the unit of a local church, separating the churches by the cities, and not establishing higher, supervisory institutions above the cities. If one local church becomes sinful or has failed, the sin and failure will not affect other churches. If God placed seven or eight churches under the rule of a few people, as soon as one or two of these few people fell, the seven or eight churches would fall as well. If God had established a headquarters in Asia to rule over the seven churches, as soon as the headquarters failed, the seven churches would have failed also. The seven churches in Asia were directly responsible to the Lord. Although five of them failed and fell, Smyrna and Philadelphia, who served as God's remnant, did not fail. God did this in order to avoid such danger. It protects weak and good churches from infiltration by sin and improper things.

THE DETERMINATION OF BOUNDARY BY THE CITY

The concept of the city was not originally in the Bible. In the beginning God created the garden of Eden, but it was not a city. In the end God will gain the New Jerusalem—a city. Hence, the concept of a city came in after man's fall. Before man fell, everything, including the tree of life and all the fruits, was in the garden of Eden. The living water flowed out of the garden of Eden. After man fell, God's work was changed from a garden to a city. A garden does not seem to have a boundary; there is no protection. God made the city for the purpose of protection, so that there were city walls for its boundary and it could be separated from other things. This separation keeps sin out. Not only does God care for the city today, in the millennium His concern will be only for the city. In the future, some will rule over five cities, while others will rule over ten cities. Not only will God care for the city in the millennium, but He will care for the city even in the new heaven and new earth. Then there will be the New Jerusalem. God exalts the city because a city has a boundary which separates it from other places. This distinction has less likelihood of confusion, and it is easy to manage.

Although we have said that the church sometimes takes a village as its boundary, a village is a miniature city in reality. God's concept is still the city. When there are a few believers meeting in a city, that meeting becomes the local church in that locality. Another church from another city cannot come and interfere with this meeting. The boundary of the church in a city is the boundary of the city. The boundary of a local church is determined by the political boundary of the city. God has not left the decision of the boundary of a local church to the brothers or the elders. The responsibility of the church is to follow the division of the government and to take the political boundary as the boundary of the church. The sphere of a local church is as big as the political boundary of the city. There are big cities and small cities. A city as big as Nineveh took three days to circle once (Jonah 3:3). But a city like Jerusalem is only six miles in radius. Bethany is a place which does not belong to Jerusalem. Jerusalem is next to Bethany (John 11:18). Jerusalem is a city; it has its boundary. Bethany is a village; it also has its boundary. This is the way the Bible distinguishes the churches—according to the political boundary. Although some places are big and some places are small, the church cannot mark its boundary according to its own idea; it must mark it according to the political division. God has not given the church the liberty to have its own way. God uses the boundary established by the government. This is the basis that the church should accept today. There is no need to have another way.

THE WAY TO SUBDIVIDE MEETINGS WITHIN A CITY

We have seen that the Bible takes a city or a village as the unit for an assembly. In Shanghai, we now have a meeting in Wen-teh Lane and another in Gordon Lane. What is the relationship between these two meetings? This is the question we have to study tonight. But we have to set this question aside for the moment and consider how the Bible divides the believers when the number meeting in a city becomes too large. At Pentecost, three thousand and then five thousand people were saved in Jerusalem (Acts 2:41; 4:4). The number was large. Jerusalem was different from Corinth. There were not many saved ones in Corinth. First Corinthians 14 mentions the whole church coming together. This means that its number was small and could come together. The church in Jerusalem could not have the whole church come together. If the whole church were to come together, they would have three thousand plus five thousand plus many other saved ones. The number was too large, and they would not have an adequate facility. Hence, we see that in Jerusalem, although the believers were together, they broke bread in the homes. There is a slight difference between the assembly in Corinth and the assembly in Jerusalem. The number meeting in the city of Corinth was small, and the believers could come together in one place. The number meeting in the city of Jerusalem was large, and the believers could not meet in one place; they could only meet from house to house. Hence, when the number in a local assembly becomes large, the one assembly can have meetings in many "homes." This is what is shown in Acts 2:46.

A church can have meetings in various "homes," but there is still just one church. Suppose there were a few dozen meetings in the city of Jerusalem. Was there one church in Jerusalem, or were there a few dozen churches? The biblical answer is "one church" because God has made the city the sphere of the church. The unit of the church is the city. In the city of Jerusalem, there was only one church. Although there were a few dozen places where the church met, the administration of the church in Jerusalem was the same among all the dozens of places. They had the same elders and deacons. An elder in the church in Jerusalem could serve as an elder in one home or in another home. He was an elder in all the meetings in Jerusalem. But he could not go to Samaria to be an elder, because the church takes the city as its boundary. This is the situation of our meetings here in Shanghai.

Politically speaking, as long as the ceded territories in the city of Shanghai exist, including the French Concession, the British Concession, and the Chinese territory, these could be considered as three cities because the three areas were under three different sets of laws. But now that all these concessions have been reclaimed, the whole of Shanghai is one city again. Although there are still different police authorities in the former French Concession and the Common Concession, legally speaking there is no further distinction. The whole city of Shanghai is now considered as one city. As such, there is only one church. Hence, the meetings in Wen-teh Lane and Gordon Lane belong to one church; there is only one table, not two tables.

When the number meeting in a place becomes large, the meetings can be held in several places. Some brothers and sisters may ask how large the number has to be before they should subdivide. What are the limitations? I have mentioned the story of the Lord distributing the loaves to the brothers.

Before the Lord distributed the loaves to the four thousand and the five thousand, He ordered the disciples to divide the crowd into fifty a row or one hundred a row. After that He had the disciples distribute the loaves (Mark 6:40). According to my personal view, we all are the Lord's flock. In order to feed the Lord's flock, it is easier if we divide the sheep into fifty or one hundred per group. There are a few additional advantages to this kind of subdivision.

First, the apostles at that time did not have the money to build big meeting halls. They could only practice according to the principle of meeting in the homes, though they might not have divided into fifty a group or one hundred a group. To subdivide themselves in this way would not pose any problem as far as the place of meeting was concerned. We would rather not have a great central place of meeting and would rather meet separately in groups of fifty and one hundred.

Second, if a few thousand or a few hundred people gathered together in one place, we would not have much time to break the bread at the bread-breaking meeting on the Lord's Day evening, and there would not be a large enough cup or bread. This shows us clearly that, at the beginning of the church age, saved ones were not breaking bread in one place. Sometimes when we have two or three hundred people breaking the bread together, we have to wait for one or two hours before we can have the bread. Some can wait, but others may not be able to wait that long. This is not a question of whether or not we should wait. It is a question of some not having the energy to wait for that long.

Third, if two or three hundred people gathered together in one place, some brothers would find it difficult to come to the meeting because of the limitation of time. If all the brothers tried to know one another, they could communicate with only one or two brothers each time. If they wanted to have more opportunity to know each other and communicate with each other, they could do it only once every few months. If that was the case, the meeting would not be able to advance. If there are only fifty or a hundred meeting in a place, it is easy for the people to communicate with each other and for the meeting to go on. It is also easy to care for the members, and the care will be adequate. If the number is too large, it is difficult to care for one another, and there is the danger of negligence. This is why we should maintain this principle.

It is for this reason that we started another meeting in Gordon Lane. The reason for starting that meeting is based on this ground. Please remember that the meeting in Gordon Lane and the meeting in Wen-teh Lane are not two churches but one church with one fellowship. We are merely subdivided into two "home" meetings. The responsible ones in Wen-teh Lane and the responsible ones in Gordon Lane are the same group of people. The serving brothers here and the serving brothers there are the same brothers. If a brother meeting in Shanghai wants to go to the meeting in Nanking, he has to have a letter of recommendation. But if he goes from the meeting in Wen-teh Lane to the meeting in Gordon Lane or vice versa, there is no need for a letter of recommendation. We hope that in the near future, there will be another meeting in Bao-shan. Bao-shan is in a different county than the county that Shanghai is in. If some brother goes to the meeting in Bao-shan, he must have a letter of recommendation because Bao-shan is another city, and the church administration in that city belongs to another unit. This situation is different than the meetings in Wen-teh Lane and Gordon Lane, which are only one unit. The offering from these two places is distributed by the same group of people, and all affairs are considered to be under one unit. The ones received by either place are approved by the same brothers and announced in both places.

THE BOUNDARY OF THE MEETINGS
IN GORDON LANE AND WEN-TEH LANE

How should we designate the boundary line between the meetings in Gordon Lane and Wen-teh Lane? Which brothers and sisters should go to the meeting in Wen-teh Lane? And which brothers and sisters should belong to the meeting in Gordon Lane? The responsible brothers among us who serve as the elders have discussed this and have made the decision to make the Soochow River the boundary line. All the brothers and sisters who reside to the north of the Soochow River should meet in Gordon Lane, and all the brothers and sisters who reside to the south of the Soochow River should meet in Wen-teh Lane. This designation does not mean that the brothers and sisters residing to the north of the Soochow River cannot meet in Wen-teh Lane or that the brothers and sisters residing to the south of the Soochow River cannot meet in Gordon Lane. It means that those residing to the north of the Soochow River should consider the meeting in Gordon Lane their meeting, and they should bear special responsibility and have special care for that meeting. Those who reside to the south of the Soochow River should consider the meeting in Wen-teh Lane their meeting, and they should bear special responsibility and have special care for that meeting. Therefore, we hope that the brothers and sisters residing to the north of the Soochow River will meet separately from the brothers and sisters residing to the south of the Soochow River. We hope that in the future, there will be meetings in the French Concession, Yang-shu-pu, and Kiang-wan also. Then we hope that the ones who are serving as elders will survey the land and decide who should break bread in each place. Presently, we have only two meeting places, and the Soochow River is the boundary. We should conduct our practice in an orderly way according to this principle.

THE BOUNDARY BEYOND THE CITY

As to the boundary line between the city and the suburb of the city, we have not yet delved into this subject. But let us consider Joshua 21:3: "And the children of Israel gave unto the Levites out of their inheritance, at the commandment of the Lord, these cities and their suburbs." This verse mentions the city and the suburbs of the city. Deuteronomy 28:3 says, "Blessed shall you be in the city, and blessed shall you be in the field." This verse mentions the city and the field. According to the Old Testament, every city has its suburbs, and every city has its fields. These suburbs and fields surround the city and sustain the city. The vegetables and staples of the city come from the suburbs and fields around it. The city cannot survive by itself. That is why there are four gates at the four sides of the city. The Bible also shows us that each city should bear the responsibility of its suburbs and fields. Therefore, the church in a city should be responsible not only for the city but for its suburbs and fields. Whether it is gospel preaching or any other kind of work, the church in the city should care for the need of the suburbs and fields around the city. The suburbs and the fields are there to support the city and increase the number of those meeting in the city. In other words, those in the church in the city should care for those living in the suburbs of the city. If anyone is saved in the suburbs, he cannot meet in the suburbs but should be brought to the meeting in the city and should support the meeting in the city so that the meeting in the city can become bigger, stronger, more prosperous, and more developed. Among us, there are brothers from Kiang-wan. Kiang-wan is like a suburb. When they come to our meeting, they are supporting the assembly in Shanghai. I am merely giving you an example. At the beginning, the assembly in the city is the center. By the time the number from the suburbs becomes large, these ones have learned to meet. When they are strong enough to set up another meeting, they may become a "home" meeting and may start meeting in the suburbs. Before that, they should come to the city for their meeting and support the meeting in the center.

THE BOUNDARY BETWEEN
ONE ASSEMBLY AND ANOTHER

At times, there are problems between two assemblies concerning their boundaries. Some people may live close to the border of two assemblies. Who should meet in Bao-shan, and who should meet in Kiang-wan? Who should meet in Wen-teh Lane, and who should meet in Gordon Lane? Who should make the decision regarding these things? We should decide according to the principle in Deuteronomy 21:2-3 and 6 concerning the slain. "Then your elders and judges shall go out and measure the distance to the cities that surround the slain man. And the city that is nearest to the slain man, that is, the elders of that city, shall take a heifer of the herd which has not been worked and has not drawn the yoke....and all the elders of that city that is nearest the slain man shall wash their hands over the heifer whose neck was broken in the river valley." The elders of the city have to come forth to measure and find out which city is closest. The responsibility will then fall on the closest city. Hence, the boundary of the assemblies is very simple. If there are clear political marks, we can mark the boundaries clearly. If there are no clear political boundaries, the elders should measure and decide to which assembly a certain area should belong. In this way, everything will become clear. Those brothers who live close to one assembly should meet with that assembly, and everyone should submit to authority in a proper way.

THE RESTRICTION OF SUBDIVIDING ONE ASSEMBLY INTO TWO LOCAL MEETINGS

When can one assembly be subdivided into two "home" meetings? It must wait until the number becomes large before subdividing into two meetings. Moreover, after the subdivision, both meetings must remain strong. It is better to have a hundred, or at least fifty or seventy-five, in each meeting after the subdivision.

We want to mention the brothers' request for a meeting in Bao-shan. At present, the brothers in Bao-shan are an outgrowth of the meeting in Gordon Lane. These brothers wrote to the brothers in Gordon Lane and wanted to start another meeting in Bao-shan and break the bread there. What should they do in order to be scriptural? They should not merely realize that it is scriptural for brothers to meet together, but they should make sure that they have the leading of the Holy Spirit and consider the condition of their meeting. They should take care of the meeting in Gordon Lane. First, they have to consider the number meeting in Gordon Lane and see whether that number is becoming too large for everyone to meet together and whether the time is ripe for them to subdivide. If the meeting in Gordon Lane is a weak meeting, a subdivision will further weaken the situation and make it even more difficult to go on. Second, we should not think that we can set up the Lord's table recklessly just because we want to break bread and remember the Lord in a place. Actually, the minute we set up the Lord's table in a place, the question of the church immediately comes up, and we have to bear the responsibility of the church. Can these brothers deal with the problem of receiving and excommunicating people? Can they be responsible to take up other burdens? Therefore, we have to pray much concerning this matter before we can have the proper answer.

Suppose it is time for the brothers in Bao-shan to start their meeting. What are the procedures? They should inform the assembly in Shanghai (both the meeting in Wen-teh Lane and the meeting in Gordon Lane) and tell it of their intention to start a meeting. Those brothers who intend to meet in Bao-shan should pray much, and the brothers in Shanghai should also pray much. If in their prayer, both sides feel with one accord that this can be done, the brothers in Bao-shan can then have their own meeting, and they will have the blessing and the laying on of hands of the brothers. This shows that the brothers in Bao-shan have received the approval of all the brothers and are not acting according to their own will. This is like bees multiplying their hives into smaller colonies. This kind of move is done in a happy way because it is done through much prayer and much fellowship with the brothers. This way is the way of the laying on of hands; it is not the way of an independent move. I have to add a few words. Even though we may meet separately in this way, it does not mean that Shanghai does not need a meeting place that is bigger than what it now has. In Shanghai we still need a meeting place that can hold five hundred or more because every year people come to our conferences from everywhere.

QUESTIONS

Question: In Taichow someone asked about the matter of the laying on of hands. Should we practice the laying on of hands today?

Answer: There is such a thing as the laying on of hands in the Bible. But it is not the so-called laying on of hands (or ordination) that men know of today. Today it is always those who are greater who lay hands on those who are smaller. But in the Bible, we find both the greater ones laying hands on the smaller ones, and the smaller ones laying hands on the greater ones. Acts 8 mentions Peter and John going to Samaria. They laid hands as the greater upon the smaller. But Acts 13 tells us that the teachers and prophets laid hands on the apostles. This is clearly a case of the smaller ones laying hands on the greater ones. In the church in Antioch we see some prophets and teachers. While they were serving the Lord and fasting, the Holy Spirit told them that they should send Barnabas and Saul out for the work which He had called them to do. They laid hands on the two and sent them out. We know that Paul and Barnabas were apostles, but the prophets and the teachers were the ones who laid hands on them. Ephesians 4 clearly puts the apostles first and the prophets and teachers second (v. 11). Acts 13 shows us that the ones who were second laid hands on the ones who were first. This shows that the laying on of hands is not an act of the greater upon the smaller, as some have imagined. In the Bible, the laying on of hands merely signifies fellowship, sympathy, and mutual union. The laying on of hands in Acts 8 indicates that the Samaritans were joined to the Body of Christ in the same way that baptism signifies one's union with the death of Christ. The laying on of hands in Acts 13 signifies that the church was joined to, sympathetic with, and in fellowship with Paul and his companion. Their going was the whole church's going. This laying on of hands shows that it was not just Paul and Barnabas who went on their missionary journey, but the whole church in Antioch went with them. It shows that their work and move were not just related to the two of them; they were related to the whole church in Antioch. The laying on of hands did not only signify their fellowship with those who laid hands on them; it also signified fellowship between the ones on whom the hands were laid and the whole church in Antioch. If any person goes out from us for some kind of work, it is best if he goes out after we lay hands on him.

We should brush aside or wipe away the dust of human tradition from biblical teachings as dust is wiped away from a mirror. Many people do not wipe away the dust. Instead, they think that the mirror is too dusty and break the mirror altogether. Many people think that talking about elders, deacons, and the laying on of hands will make us the same as the denominations. Actually, the original thing was not wrong; what was added later is wrong. Our goal is not to destroy the work of the denominations but to recover what God has ordained in the beginning. We cannot throw away the examples in the Bible just because all the other things are wrong. Our aim is to ask whether God has commanded something. When I go out to work, many times I wish that the brothers would lay hands on me. This shows that I am not going out alone but being sent by the whole assembly, and the whole assembly is sympathetic to what I am doing. I hope those who serve as elders among us would practice the laying on of hands in the future.

Question: Paul imparted gifts to Timothy through the laying on of hands (2 Tim. 1:6). Does this not mean that gifts come from the laying on of hands?

Answer: What is a gift? It is the capacity of a member in the Body. In other words, if you are an eye in the Body, your gift is your capacity to see. If you are an ear in the Body, your gift is your capacity to hear. When a man is joined to the Body of Christ, he immediately receives a gift. The laying on of hands by the apostles is their acknowledgment of a person as being a member of the Body of Christ on behalf of the Body of Christ. It pleases God to manifest man's gift after such an act. Acts 13 also signifies a union with the Body of Christ. In Acts 13 the laying on of hands was not to manifest a gift but to express that they were all co-workers together. There was never a case in which prophets and teachers imparted gifts to the apostles. As to the miraculous gifts in the Bible, they should be present with us and should not be something of the past. I do not understand why there are no miraculous gifts today. The practice of the laying on of hands should not stop with us. Paul told Timothy that he should not lay hands on others quickly lest he partake of their sins (1 Tim. 5:22). Hebrews 6 tells us that we do not have to lay a foundation again. Such a foundation includes baptism and the laying on of hands (vv. 1-2). Hence, if we neglect the matter of the laying on of hands, we must have erred in the foundational matters. Of course, we cannot impart gifts by our laying on of hands as it was practiced in the days of the apostles; today we are merely practicing the principle. We admit that we are like the church in Philadelphia; we do not have much strength. All we have is a little strength (Rev. 3:8).

Question: At present, we have two meetings. How should the responsibility and work be distributed between the two meetings?

Answer: In the meetings in Gordon Lane and Wen-teh Lane, we should have two or three elders take charge of everything. There should also be a few deacons or deaconesses in the meeting in Gordon Lane, just as there are some in Wen-teh Lane. We mentioned the work in the brothers' meeting last Saturday. We will have prayer meetings in Gordon Lane the same way that we have prayer meetings here. For the sake of the work in the future, we hope that the brothers meeting in Gordon Lane can rent a larger place. If we want to start any work there, the present rented place is too small. In the future, we may separate the Lord's Day morning and afternoon meeting. We may meet in Gordon Lane in the morning and in Wen-teh Lane in the afternoon. We may even have the two places take turns holding the brothers' meeting and the sisters' meeting. Perhaps we will have them in one place one week and in another place another week. Otherwise, some will think that the meeting in Gordon Lane is the branch church of the meeting in Wen-teh Lane. Some have asked me if the meeting in Gordon Lane is a branch of the meeting in Wen-teh Lane. I told them it is not. The meeting in Wen-teh Lane is the same as the meeting in Gordon Lane.

Question: Should we not say "the meeting *in* Gordon Lane" and "the meeting *in* Wen-teh Lane" instead of saying "the Gordon Lane meeting" and "the Wen-teh Lane meeting"?

Answer: Yes, we should.

Question: If in the future we decide to start a meeting in Bao-shan, should we inform all the other brothers?

Answer: We should inform both meetings. First, we should inform the meeting in Gordon Lane. Then we should inform the meeting in Wen-teh Lane. We should ask the brothers and sisters in both meetings to pray for this matter until they have the full assurance after their prayer. Then the brothers in Bao-shan can be given a definite answer. This is the best and most proper way.

Question: Concerning the matter of receiving others for the bread-breaking meeting, if the brothers in Gordon Lane are not clear about receiving a brother, can they ask the brothers meeting in Wen-teh Lane about this?

Answer: The elders in both places are the same group of elders. Therefore, Wen-teh Lane does not have anything more than what Gordon Lane has. When we receive a person, the "elders" in Shanghai, together with all the brothers, receive such a one; there is no difference whether the person is received in Wen-teh Lane or Gordon Lane. Concerning the matter of receiving a person, we have to practice it in a proper way in the future. Romans 14:1 says, "Now him who is weak in faith receive," and 15:7 says, "Therefore receive one another, as Christ also received you to the glory of God." Receiving is only part of the procedure. The question is whether or not a man has the faith. We ask whether a person has faith; we do not ask whether his faith is strong or weak. Moreover, the question is whether or not God has received him. Therefore, we have to be clear whether God has received such a one. If God has not received him, we cannot receive him either.

CONCERNING RECEIVING

Concerning the matter of receiving, I have to mention a few things.

Those Recommended by Letters from Another Locality

Those from another locality who come with a letter of recommendation should be received by us. But we have to know from where the letter of recommendation came. If it is a letter of recommendation from the denominations, we will not know whether he is clear about the truth and whether he is saved. Hence, those who are recommended by places that we do not know cannot be received by us based on a letter. But if it is a letter written by an assembly such as the one in Hangchow, we can trust in such a recommendation and receive the recommended person. We should trust that what Hangchow does is the same as what we do.

Those Recommended by the Testimony of Two or Three

If two or three brothers testify for and recommend a certain brother to the bread-breaking meeting, we can receive this one. There is a problem among us today of how to receive transient visitors. They pass by us on their way to other places and intend to break bread only once with us. This is difficult to handle. There are also members of some denominations who break bread with us but return to the denominations to break bread there. This is also difficult to handle. In my opinion, it is best to have two or three brothers talk with these ones immediately to check whether they are saved and then decide whether we will receive them for the bread. We cannot ask these people to wait until the next week before we answer them. They are not like those who intend to have long-term fellowship with us, whom we can ask to wait a little.

Three Kinds of Letters of Recommendation

The letters of recommendation which we send out should be of three kinds: (1) those that recommend a brother as one who has not left the denominations yet; (2) those that recommend a brother as one who is standing on the ground of the church; and (3) those that recommend a brother as one who has some gifts.

A Few Things One Should Know in Recommending Someone to Break Bread

(1) We should ask whether such a one is saved or not. (2) We should know whether he commits the sins worthy of excommunication as recorded in 1 Corinthians 5. (3) We should show him that the breaking of bread is not only for the remembrance of the Lord, but for the discerning of the Body of Christ and for taking a stand in the Body of Christ. The first two matters are the conditions; a man must be saved and must be clean. The third is the teaching; a person must be

able to discern the Body of Christ and must take the stand of the Body of Christ. If he does not discern such things, in God's eyes he eats judgment for his sins to himself (1 Cor. 11:29). If he does this, the breaking of bread will not be of much benefit to him.

If a man is saved and has not committed the sins of 1 Corinthians 5 but does not see the truth about discerning the Body, we must still receive him because we have to receive those who are weak in the faith. I think we have not been faithful to those who visit us from the denominations. We have not told them the importance before God of discerning the Body. We should show them this point. However, if we make the discerning of the Body a condition for receiving a person, we become a sect. This is why we have to be careful. However, we should not forget the teaching of Titus 3:10.

Questions

Question: After a person is saved, does he have to wait until he is baptized before he can break the bread?

Answer: It is best for a saved person to be baptized before taking the bread. In the Bible, there is no such thing as believing first and then waiting for a long time before being baptized; believing and baptism are always linked together. There is no such thing as putting a man aside for a few months after he is saved and then baptizing such a one. Such a practice is not found in the New Testament. But we should not make baptism a condition for partaking of the bread. Some have only been sprinkled and do not know that baptism is a testimony. We should still receive them for the bread-breaking meeting. Those from the Salvation Army do not believe in baptism at all, and none of them are baptized. The Quakers, particularly those who are in China, do not have baptism and bread-breaking at all. There are other smaller denominations which believe the same way as the Quakers. If these people come to us, we should receive them. Since God has received them, we should receive them also. We should receive those who are weak in faith. We can receive them because they belong to God. We cannot make baptism a condition for receiving a person; we can only consider baptism a teaching. Neither should we excommunicate those who are not baptized. When a person sees the cross, he will spontaneously be baptized and obey this truth.

Question: The meetings in Gordon Lane and Wen-teh Lane are actually one assembly and are one. In receiving a visitor, should one meeting inform the other of such?

Answer: If it can be done practically, one should inform the other concerning the receiving of a visitor. But if it cannot be done practically, there is no need to inform the other meeting. If anyone wants to remain with us for a long time, those who serve as elders in either meeting should stand on the ground of the church and discuss the matter properly before making a decision. This is why the announcements made in the prayer meeting in Gordon Lane should also be made in the prayer meeting in Wen-teh Lane and vice versa so that there can be prayers in one accord. I hope that the meeting in Gordon Lane can install a telephone. When this happens, it will be easier to discuss matters between the two places.

OTHER BOOKS PUBLISHED BY
Living Stream Ministry

Titles by Witness Lee:

Abraham—Called by God	978-0-7363-0359-0
The Experience of Life	978-0-87083-417-2
The Knowledge of Life	978-0-87083-419-6
The Tree of Life	978-0-87083-300-7
The Economy of God	978-0-87083-415-8
The Divine Economy	978-0-87083-268-0
God's New Testament Economy	978-0-87083-199-7
The World Situation and God's Move	978-0-87083-092-1
Christ vs. Religion	978-0-87083-010-5
The All-inclusive Christ	978-0-87083-020-4
Gospel Outlines	978-0-87083-039-6
Character	978-0-87083-322-9
The Secret of Experiencing Christ	978-0-87083-227-7
The Life and Way for the Practice of the Church Life	978-0-87083-785-2
The Basic Revelation in the Holy Scriptures	978-0-87083-105-8
The Crucial Revelation of Life in the Scriptures	978-0-87083-372-4
The Spirit with Our Spirit	978-0-87083-798-2
Christ as the Reality	978-0-87083-047-1
The Central Line of the Divine Revelation	978-0-87083-960-3
The Full Knowledge of the Word of God	978-0-87083-289-5
Watchman Nee—A Seer of the Divine Revelation ...	978-0-87083-625-1

Titles by Watchman Nee:

How to Study the Bible	978-0-7363-0407-8
God's Overcomers	978-0-7363-0433-7
The New Covenant	978-0-7363-0088-9
The Spiritual Man • 3 volumes	978-0-7363-0269-2
Authority and Submission	978-0-7363-0185-5
The Overcoming Life	978-1-57593-817-2
The Glorious Church	978-0-87083-745-6
The Prayer Ministry of the Church	978-0-87083-860-6
The Breaking of the Outer Man and the Release ...	978-1-57593-955-1
The Mystery of Christ	978-1-57593-954-4
The God of Abraham, Isaac, and Jacob	978-0-87083-932-0
The Song of Songs	978-0-87083-872-9
The Gospel of God • 2 volumes	978-1-57593-953-7
The Normal Christian Church Life	978-0-87083-027-3
The Character of the Lord's Worker	978-1-57593-322-1
The Normal Christian Faith	978-0-87083-748-7
Watchman Nee's Testimony	978-0-87083-051-8

Available at
Christian bookstores, or contact Living Stream Ministry
2431 W. La Palma Ave. • Anaheim, CA 92801
1-800-549-5164 • www.livingstream.com